# MARY FORD
## ONE HUNDRED
## EASY CAKE
## DESIGNS

# MARY FORD
# ONE HUNDRED EASY CAKE DESIGNS

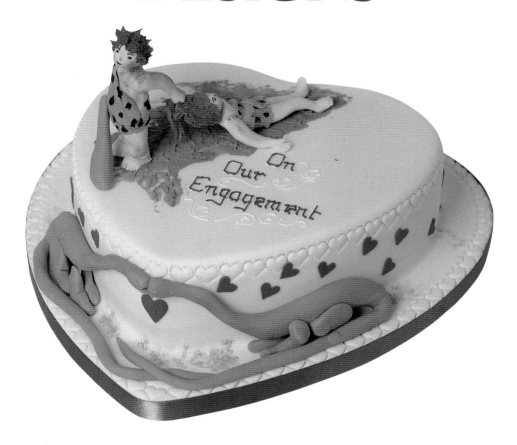

## MARY FORD

# A MARY FORD BOOK

Published 1995 by Mary Ford Publications Limited,
99 Spring Road, Tyseley, Birmingham B11 3DJ England.

Typesetting by Russ Design & Production, Salisbury.

ISBN 0 946429 47 2

# THE AUTHOR

For over twenty five years, Mary Ford's personal warmth and expertise in her craft have endeared her to students and cake-decorating enthusiasts from all around the world. Now, through her immensely popular step-by-step teaching books, busy mothers and novice decorators are being introduced to Mary's imaginative and yet simple approach to decoration.

Mary's life is dedicated to bringing the pleasure of cake artistry to an ever increasing audience. Her professional expertise and innovative skills, combined with many years of practical teaching experience, allow her to reach everyone, no matter what their age and experience. Her enthusiasm and patience are such that she is never too busy to answer a reader's query, and her attention to detail reflects the care and concern that go into designing and crafting her books and the cakes that are featured in them.

Mary is helped in this work by her husband Michael, who is both the photographer and executive director for her publications.

## ACKNOWLEDGEMENTS

With grateful thanks to Mary Smith and Dawn Pennington.

Cakeboards Limited, 47-53 Dace Road, London, E3 2NH. Manufacturers and suppliers of cake decorating equipment and decorations to the wholesale and retail trade.

Orchard Products, 51 Hallyburton Road, Hove, East Sussex, BN3 7GP. Manufacturers and suppliers of cake decorating equipment to the retail trade and by mail order.

# CONTENTS

NOTE: WHEN MAKING ANY OF THE RECIPES IN THIS BOOK, FOLLOW ONE SET OF MEASUREMENTS ONLY AS THEY ARE NOT INTERCHANGEABLE.

# INTRODUCTION

I am delighted to introduce my 100 Easy Cake Designs.

Cake artistry is a very pleasurable activity. Whether you are looking for an occasional idea, or inspiration for an absorbing hobby, my intention is to start you creating. For this reason, I have chosen designs that do not require a high standard of skill or finish. You can begin immediately, and your reward will be a stunning cake.

I have used decorating aids such as sugarpaste figures and cut-outs, rice paper, piping gel, jelly sweets and a variety of artificial decorations as well as the more traditional piping techniques and sugarpaste flowers that will appeal to experienced decorators. Some of the cakes are so simple that anyone can make them, young or old. It is never too soon to start learning. Children love working with sugarpaste and even the youngest can draw onto rice paper with food approved pens, and teenagers will find inspiration and practical techniques for a cake to surprise Mum or Dad. To save time, you can buy ready-made almond and sugarpaste (available in supermarkets and craft shops) and ready-to-mix royal icing.

One of the secrets of a beautiful cake is the planning that goes into it. Where appropriate, decide on the basic cake: fruit or sponge. Always read through the instructions carefully and have everything to hand when you are ready to begin. Timing is important. Work backwards from the date the cake is needed. Enough time must be allowed for a fruit cake to mature; about three weeks. Coatings and piping need to dry. Items need to be purchased.

The quality of the basic cake is important. No amount of decorating will hide a cake that is disappointing in taste or texture. For this reason, the preliminary section of this book includes tried and tested recipes for cakes and coatings that ensure success. All sizes and shapes of cake are included and easy-to-follow tables enable you to select exactly the right size for your needs.

This is followed by a step-by-step practical guide to coating and covering cakes. A good finish is much easier to work on so it is worth taking the time to study this section carefully if you are new to cake decorating.

The 100 designs for every occasion in this book offer exciting possibilities for everyone. As always, each design is set out pictorially for you to follow step-by-step. However, experienced decorators will soon find opportunities for combining and adapting designs for different situations.

I do hope, as always, that these designs will fire your imagination and open up the exciting world of cake artistry for you.

Marytord

# GUIDELINES

### FIXING

Apricot purée can be used to fix cake to cake or almond paste to cake. Buttercream can be used to join sponge cakes.
Always use cooled, boiled water or clear liquor when fixing sugarpaste to sugarpaste.
Use royal icing to fix royal icing or runouts.
Ribbons should be fixed with small dots or fine lines of royal icing.

### PIPING GEL

Most sugarcraft outlets stock clear piping gel which may be easily coloured using liquid or paste food colourings. Many supermarkets also stock ready made tubes of coloured piping gel.
Use a small piping bag without a tube for piping. Do not overfill the bag. Outline each section with royal icing before filling with piping gel. A little piping gel can go a very long way.

### CAKE BOARDS

Always use strong, thick cake boards for fruit cakes to prevent damage when moving.
If using decorative paper to cover a board, glue the paper to the board. It is essential to then place a thin cake card between the cake and the decorative paper.

### COLOURS

Always prepare sufficient coloured sugarpaste or icing to complete the work as it is virtually impossible to match the colour later.

### TIERING

Cake stands can be hired which will avoid the need for pillars. If pillars are required for royal iced cakes, see the table on page 21.

# EQUIPMENT

Before beginning work, it is vital to make sure that you have all the equipment you need. All utensils should be scrupulously clean and free from grease. The right equipment makes the work much easier, and more enjoyable. However, with a little ingenuity, equipping yourself need not be expensive. Much of what you need will already be found in your kitchen and it is possible to improvise and still achieve excellent results. An electric mixer will prove to be a great bonus and will save time and energy, although it is by no means essential for success.

If you do buy equipment, always look for quality. Careful buying will ensure that the utensils will last a lifetime. Inferior items will rust, bend and chip and, therefore, will be a false economy. Buy food-approved spoons and plastic bowls and, where possible, keep these for decorating. Stainless steel items are ideal, other metals should be avoided as they may discolour icing. Glass and earthenware containers should be free from cracks. Cake tins come in a variety of sizes and shapes but should be strong and rigid. It is also possible to hire specially shaped tins for unusual cakes. Ovenproof pudding basins for baking round cakes are easily obtainable. It is also worth spending money on good quality greaseproof paper.

A decorating turntable makes all the difference when working on a cake and a small one can be improvised using an upturned cake tin or a plate. However, if you decorate cakes regularly, a proper turntable is a wise investment and makes the task much easier. The turntable should be capable of supporting a heavy cake and still turn easily when in use. It should have a non slip-base and a minimum diameter of 23cm (9in).

You will need a good quality rolling pin that is smooth and heavy 45cm (18in) long. Smaller plastic rolling pins can also be useful. Nylon spacers ensure an even thickness of paste.

Two stainless steel palette knives are required for mixing-in colour and coating cakes. An 18cm (7in) and a 10cm (4in) will be enough to cope with most tasks. You will also need a stainless steel or rigid plastic straight edge that is at least 38cm (15in) long for smoothing royal icing and buttercream.

Coating cake-sides is best done with a purpose made rigid plastic or stainless steel side scraper, available from specialist cake-decorating shops.

Piping tubes may be plastic or metal and come in a wide variety of different sizes (see Glossary). Tubes should always be washed immediately after use to prevent icing hardening inside.

Flower cutters, wires, crimpers and other specialised equipment is available from sugarcraft shops or by mail-order.

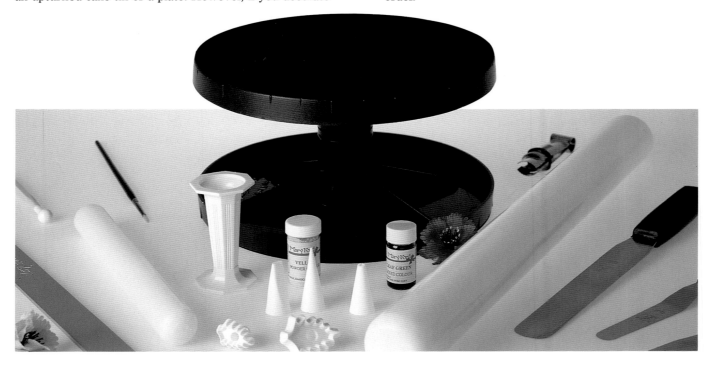

# WHITWORTHS

For over 100 years Whitworths have been sourcing premium quality ingredients from around the world for people to use in baking and decorating cakes.

Dried Fruits, sourced from as far away as Australia and America, fall into two categories:

Dried Vine Fruits – Currants, Sultanas and Raisins are all made by taking whole bunches of Grapes from the grapevine and laying them out to dry naturally under the warmth of the sun. The resultant Dried Fruit is a source of minerals (including Calcium, Iron and Copper) and Vitamins, particularly A and B groups.

Dried Tree Fruits, are equally as nutritious as the Dried Vine Fruits. An extensive range is available offering the old baking favourites such as Dates, either sugar rolled ready chopped or whole, and Figs. Dried Plums, commonly referred to as Prunes, Apricots, Apple Rings, Pears and Peaches can be added in place of traditional Vine Fruits, to bake interesting cakes. Dried Banana Chips are great for decorating cakes or sprinkling over ice cream and puddings.

Glacé Fruits, are additional favourite store cupboard ingredients. Whitworths source only the finest Bigarreaux Cherries, grown in the Provence region of France and acknowledged to be the finest Glacé Cherries in the world.

Nuts play an important role in homebaking. In the past, Nuts tended to be used for their crunchy texture and flavour alone, but now they are recognised for their high nutritional value. Nuts are rich in Protein as well as Calcium, Vitamin B and Iron. All nuts must be stored in a cool dry place to ensure that they do not become oily or rancid.

The most popular Nut for baking is the Sweet Almond. Sweet Almonds are available whole blanched, flaked, chopped or ground and are ideal in cakes, biscuits and puddings.

Hazelnuts, sometimes called Filberts, are closely related to Cob Nuts. Either chopped or ground they can be added to cakes, pastries or puddings. The brown skins can be removed from Hazelnuts although the skins do look attractive when the whole nuts are used as a decoration.

Chopped mixed Nuts are handy for cake decorating and creating a crunchy texture for sauces and over ice cream.

Desiccated Coconut is produced by shredding the whitemeat of coconut and leaving it to dry in the sun. It can be toasted or coloured and used to flavour or decorate cakes or biscuits.

Using only the finest quality Almonds and Icing Sugar, Whitworths produce both Golden and White Marzipan to provide cake makers with an easy to use product for applying to cakes or modelling.

Whitworths were the innovators in the Ready-To-Roll Icing market, creating a delicious fondant Icing that takes the hard work out of cake covering. Unopened, the Icing will keep satisfactorily for months as long as it is kept in a cool place.

As an alternative to eloborate Icing techniques, a multitude of attractive ingredients are available under the Topits range. Multi-coloured Sugar Strands, Hundreds and Thousands, Chocolate Chips, Jelly Diamonds and Orange and Lemon Slices are just some of the prodcts that will bring fun and colour to cakes, ice cream and home-made desserts.

# ALL-IN-ONE SPONGE CAKE

This sponge is ideal for birthday cakes and cutting into shapes for novelty cakes.
For hexagonal, octagonal or petal shaped sponges use recipes for the equivalent round sponge. Example, for 20.5cm (8in) heart shape use ingredients for 20.5cm (8in) round sponge.

**SPONGE TIN SHAPES**   **SPONGE TIN SIZES**

| SPONGE TIN SHAPES | | | | | | |
|---|---|---|---|---|---|---|
| ROUND | 15cm (6in) | 18cm (7in) | 20.5cm (8in) | 23cm (9in) | 25.5cm (10in) | 28cm (11in) |
| SQUARE | 12.5cm (5in) | 15cm (6in) | 18cm (7in) | 20.5cm (8in) | 23cm (9in) | 25.5cm (10in) |
| PUDDING BASIN | 450ml (¾pt) | 600ml (1pt) | 750ml (1¼pt) | 900ml (1½pt) | 1 litre (1¾pt) | 1.2 Litre (2pt) |
| LOAF TIN | | 18.5 x 9 x 5cm 450g (1lb) | | | 21.5 x 11 x 6cm 900g (2lb) | |
| Self-raising flour | 45g (1½oz) | 60g (2oz) | 85g (3oz) | 115g (4oz) | 170g (6oz) | 225g (8oz) |
| Baking powder | ¼tsp | ½tsp | ¾tsp | 1tsp | 1½tsp | 2tsp |
| Soft (tub) margarine | 45g (1½oz) | 60g (2oz) | 85g (3oz) | 115g (4oz) | 170g (6oz) | 225g (8oz) |
| Caster sugar | 45g (1½oz) | 60g (2oz) | 85g (3oz) | 115g (4oz) | 170g (6oz) | 225g (8oz) |
| Eggs | 1 size 4 | 1 size 3 | 1 size 1 | 2 size 3 | 3 size 3 | 4 size 3 |
| Baking temperature | ------------------------ 170°C (325°F) or Gas Mark 3 ------------------------ | | | | | |
| Approximate baking time | 20 min | 25 mins | 30 mins | 32 mins | 35 mins | 40 mins |

PLEASE NOTE: Baking times for sponges baked in pudding basins and loaf tins may take longer.

---

**BAKING TEST** When the sponge has reached the recommended baking time, open the oven door slowly and, if the sponge is pale in colour, continue baking until light brown. When light brown, run your fingers across the top gently and the sponge should spring back when touched. If not then continue baking and test every few minutes.

**FREEZING** Sponge cake can be frozen for up to six months. Make sure that it is completely thawed before use.

**STORAGE** Use within three days of baking or defrosting.

**PORTIONS** A 20.5cm (8in) round sponge should provide approximately sixteen portions when decorated.

**For chocolate flavoured sponges:**

For every 115g (4oz) of flour used in the recipe add 2tbsp of cocoa powder dissolved in 2tbsp of hot water, leave to cool then add to the other ingredients in step 3.

**For coffee flavoured sponges:**

For every 115g (4oz) of flour used in the recipe add 2tsp of instant coffee dissolved in 1tbsp of boiling water, leave to cool then add to the other ingredients in step 3.

**For orange or lemon flavoured sponges:**

For every 115g (4oz) of flour used in the recipe add the grated rind of one orange or lemon to the other ingredients in step 3.

**INGREDIENTS** *for Two 20.5cm round sponges (8in) or two 18cm square sponges (7in).*

170g self-raising flour (6oz)
1½ tsp baking powder
170g soft (tub) margarine (6oz)
170g caster sugar (6oz)
3 eggs, size 3

## BAKING

Bake in a pre-heated oven at 170°C (325°F) or Gas Mark 3 for approximately 30 minutes.

## EQUIPMENT

Two 20.5cm round sponge tins (8in)
OR two 18cm square sponge tins (7in)
Soft (tub) margarine for greasing
Brush
Greaseproof paper
Mixing bowl
Sieve
Beater
Spatula

1 Grease the tins with soft (tub) margarine, line the bases with greaseproof paper then grease the paper.

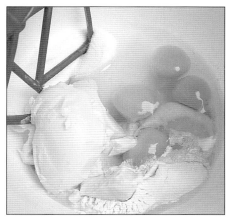

2 Sift the flour and baking powder together twice to ensure a thorough mix. Then place into a mixing bowl with all the other ingredients.

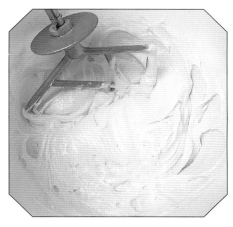

3 Beat mixture for 3-4 minutes until light in colour.

4 Spread the mixture evenly between the two tins. Bake in pre-heated oven (see baking test).

5 When the sponges are baked, leave to cool in the tins for 5 minutes, then carefully turn out onto a wire tray until cold.

6 When cold, sandwich the sponges together with jam and cream then place into a refrigerator for 1 hour before decorating.

# ALL-IN-ONE FRUIT CAKE

This fruit cake makes the ideal base for any sugarpaste or royal icing celebration cake and has excellent keeping properties. When making a fruit cake, it requires at least three weeks to mature.

For hexagonal, octagonal or petal shaped cakes use recipe for the equivalent round cake. Example, for 20.5cm (8in) heart shape use ingredients for 20.5cm (8in) round cake.

| Square tin | 12.5cm (5in) | 15cm (6in) | 18cm (7in) | 20.5cm (8in) | 23cm (9in) | 25.5cm (10in) | 28cm (11in) |
|---|---|---|---|---|---|---|---|
| OR | | | | | | | |
| Round tin | 15cm (6in) | 18cm (7in) | 20.5cm (8in) | 23cm (9in) | 25.5cm (10in) | 28cm (11in) | 30.5cm (12in) |
| Sultanas | 85g (3oz) | 115g (4oz) | 170g (6oz) | 225g (8oz) | 285g (10oz) | 340g (12oz) | 425g (15oz) |
| Currants | 85g (3oz) | 115g (4oz) | 170g (6oz) | 225g (8oz) | 285g (10oz) | 340g (12oz) | 425g (15oz) |
| Raisins | 85g (3oz) | 115g (4oz) | 170g (6oz) | 225g (8oz) | 285g (10oz) | 340g (12oz) | 425g (15oz) |
| Candied peel | 30g (1oz) | 60g (2oz) | 60g (2oz) | 85g (3oz) | 85g (3oz) | 115g (4oz) | 170g (6oz) |
| Glacé cherries | 30g (1oz) | 60g (2oz) | 60g (2oz) | 85g (3oz) | 85g (3oz) | 115g (4oz) | 170g (6oz) |
| Lemon rind (lemons) | ¼ | ½ | ½ | 1 | 1½ | 2 | 2 |
| Rum/Brandy | ½tbsp | ½tbsp | 1tbsp | 1tbsp | 1½tbsp | 2tbsp | 2tbsp |
| Black treacle | ½tbsp | ½tbsp | 1tbsp | 1tbsp | 1½tbsp | 2tbsp | 2tbsp |
| Soft (tub) margarine | 85g (3oz) | 115g (4oz) | 170g (6oz) | 225g (8oz) | 285g (10oz) | 340g (12oz) | 425g (15oz) |
| Soft light brown sugar | 85g (3oz) | 115g (4oz) | 170g (6oz) | 225g (8oz) | 285g (10oz) | 340g (12oz) | 425g (15oz) |
| Eggs, size 3 | 1½ | 2 | 3 | 4 | 5 | 6 | 7½ |
| Ground almonds | 15g (½oz) | 30g (1oz) | 45g (1½oz) | 60g (2oz) | 70g (2½oz) | 85g (3oz) | 115g (4oz) |
| Self-raising flour | 115g (4oz) | 145g (5oz) | 200g (7oz) | 255g (9oz) | 315g (11oz) | 400g (14oz) | 515g (18oz) |
| Ground mace | pinch | pinch | pinch | pinch | pinch | pinch | pinch |
| Mixed spice | ¼tsp | ½tsp | ½tsp | ¾tsp | 1tsp | 1¼tsp | 1½tsp |
| Ground nutmeg | pinch | pinch | ¼tsp | ¼tsp | ½tsp | ½tsp | ¾tsp |
| Baking temperature | ----150°C (300°F) or Gas Mark 2--- | | | ----------140°C (275°F) or Gas Mark 1----------- | | | |
| Approximate baking time | 1¾hrs | 2hrs | 2½hrs | 3hrs | 3½hrs | 4½hrs | 6hrs |

**BAKING TEST** Bring the cake forward from the oven at the end of the recommended baking time so that it can be tested. Insert a stainless steel skewer into the centre of the cake and slowly withdraw it. If the cake is sufficiently baked, the skewer will come out as clean as it went in. Continue baking at the same temperature if the cake mixture clings to the skewer. Test in the same way every ten minutes until the skewer is clean when withdrawn from the cake.

## INGREDIENTS

225g sultanas (8oz)
225g currants (8oz)
225g raisins (8oz)
85g candied peel (3oz)
85g glacé cherries (3oz)
1 lemon
1tbsp rum/brandy
1tbsp black treacle

225g soft (tub) margarine (8oz)
225g soft light brown sugar (8oz)
4 eggs, size 3
60g ground almonds (2oz)
255g self-raising flour (9oz)
Pinch of ground mace
¾tsp mixed spice
¼tsp ground nutmeg

## EQUIPMENT

20.5cm square cake tin (8in)
OR 23cm round cake tin (9in)
Soft (tub) margarine for greasing
Greaseproof paper
Mixing bowl
Beater
Sieve
Mixing spoon
Skewer

## PREPARATION of INGREDIENTS

Weigh all the ingredients separately. Chop cherries in half and carefully clean and remove stalks from all the fruit. Grate the lemon and then mix all the fruit together with rum/brandy. Sift the flour, nutmeg, spice and mace together three times. For better results leave overnight in a warm place 18°C (65°F).

## PREPARATION of the CAKE TIN

Cut out a length of greasproof paper deeper than the cake tin (enough to cover inside) and then cut along bottom edges at 2.5cm (1in) intervals. Cut a circle or square as required for the base of the tin.
Brush the inside of the tin with soft margarine. Then cover the side with greaseproof paper and place the circle or square into the bottom of the tin. Finally brush the greaseproof paper with margarine.

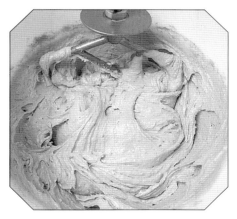  

1 Prepare the tin, fruit and other ingredients as described above. Pre-heat the oven. Place all ingredients, except the fruit, into a mixing bowl. Beat together for 2-3 minutes.

2 Using a spoon, blend in the fruit until well mixed. Place mixture into the tin, level the top and bake.

3 After recommended baking time follow baking test instructions. When baked, leave in the tin until cold. See instructions for storage.

## BAKING

Bake in a pre-heated oven at 140°C (275°F) or Gas mark 1 for approximately 2½ to 3hrs.

## STORAGE
Remove the cake carefully from the tin when it is cold and then take off the greaseproof paper. Wrap the cake in waxed paper and leave in a cupboard for at least three weeks.

## PORTIONS
To estimate the number of portions that can be cut from a finished cake, add up the total weight of all the cake ingredients, almond paste, sugarpaste and/or royal icing. As the average slice of a finished cake weighs approximately 60g (2oz), simply divide the total weight accordingly to calculate the number of portions.

# MADEIRA SPONGE CAKE

For hexagonal, octagonal or petal shaped madeira cakes use recipe for the equivalent round cake. Example, for 20.5cm (8in) heart shape use ingredients for 20.5cm (8in) round sponge cake.

| Square tin OR | 12.5cm (5in) | 15cm (6in) | 18cm (7in) | 20.5cm (8in) | 23cm (9in) | 25.5cm (10in) | 28cm (11in) |
|---|---|---|---|---|---|---|---|
| Round tin | 15cm (6in) | 18cm (7in) | 20.5cm (8in) | 23cm (9in) | 25.5cm (10in) | 28cm (11in) | 30.5cm (12in) |
| Butter | 60g (2oz) | 115g (4oz) | 170g (6oz) | 225g (8oz) | 285g (10oz) | 340g (12oz) | 400g (14oz) |
| Caster sugar | 60g (2oz) | 115g (4oz) | 170g (6oz) | 225g (8oz) | 285g (10oz) | 340g (12oz) | 400g (14oz) |
| Eggs, size 2 | 1 | 2 | 3 | 4 | 5 | 6 | 7 |
| Plain flour | 30g (1oz) | 60g (2oz) | 85g (3oz) | 115g (4oz) | 145g (5oz) | 170g (6oz) | 200g (7oz) |
| Self-raising flour | 60g (2oz) | 115g (4oz) | 170g (6oz) | 225g (8oz) | 285g (10oz) | 340g (12oz) | 400g (14oz) |
| Lemons | ¼ | ½ | 1 | 1 | 1½ | 1½ | 2 |
| Baking temperature | ----- 170°C (325°F) or Gas Mark 3 ----- | | | | | | |
| Approximate baking time | ¾hr | 1hr | 1¼hrs | 1¼hrs | 1¼hrs | 1½hrs | 1½hrs |

## CURDLING

Curdling can occur if eggs are added too quickly to the cake mixture or if there is insufficient beating between the additions. If curdling does occur, immediately beat in a small amount of flour until the batter is smooth and then continue adding egg, a little at a time. Should curdling re-occur simply add a little more flour.

BAKING TEST Bring the cake forward in the oven at the end of the recommended baking time so that it can be tested. Insert a stainless steel skewer into the centre of the cake and slowly withdraw it. If the cake is sufficiently baked, the skewer will come out of the cake as cleanly as it went in. Continue baking at the same temperature if the cake mixture clings to the skewer. Test every ten minutes until the skewer is clean when withdrawn from the cake.

FREEZING Madeira sponge cake can be frozen for up to six months. Make sure that it is completely thawed before use.

STORAGE Use within three days of baking or defrosting.

PORTIONS A 20.5cm (8in) round madeira sponge cake should serve approximately sixteen portions when decorated.

## INGREDIENTS

170g butter (6oz)
170g caster sugar (6oz)
3 eggs, size 2
85g plain flour (3oz)
170g self-raising flour (6oz)
1 lemon

## EQUIPMENT

18cm square cake tin (7in)
OR 20.5cm round cake tin (8in)
Butter for greasing
Greaseproof paper
Mixing bowl
Mixing spoon
Spatula

## BAKING

Bake in a pre-heated oven at 170°C (325°F)
or Gas Mark 3 for 1¼hrs.

1 Grease the tin lightly with butter, fully line with greaseproof paper, then grease the paper.

2 Sift the flours together. Cream the butter and sugar together until light and fluffy.

3 Stir the egg(s) together before beating a little at a time into the creamed mixture (see curdling).

4 Lightly fold the sifted flours into the mixture together with the lemon rind and juice.

5 Place mixture into the tin, and using a spatula, level the top. Bake for recommended time.

6 See baking test instructions. When baked, leave in the tin to cool for 10 minutes before turning out onto a wire rack to cool completely.

# SWISS ROLL

## INGREDIENTS

85g soft (tub) margarine (3oz)
170g caster sugar (6oz)
3 eggs, size 3
170g self-raising flour, sifted (6oz)

## EQUIPMENT

33 x 23cm swiss roll tin (13 x 9in)
Soft (tub) margarine for greasing
Greaseproof paper
Mixing bowl
Beater
Cranked (step) palette knife
Damp tea towel
Caster sugar for dusting

## BAKING

Bake in pre-heated oven at 200°C (400°F) or Gas Mark 6, for 10-12 minutes on the middle shelf.

## CHOCOLATE SWISS ROLL

For chocolate swiss roll dissolve 3 level tbsp of cocoa powder in 3tbsp hot water, leave to cool and add to the above ingredients.

## Suggested fillings:

Preserves with a little rum, brandy or liqueur added. Buttercream with the addition of any of the following: melted chocolate, chopped nuts, fresh lemon or orange, chopped glacé fruits.

## FREEZING

Roll up the sponge before freezing and store unfilled for up to six months. It should be completely thawed before unrolling.

1 Grease the swiss roll tin with melted margarine, line with greaseproof paper then grease the paper.

2 Place all the ingredients into a mixing bowl and beat for 2-3 minutes or until well mixed.

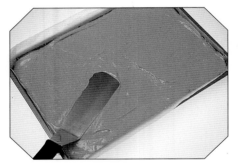

3 Spread mixture into the tin evenly. Whilst baking place greaseproof paper, slightly larger than the tin, onto a damp tea-towel.

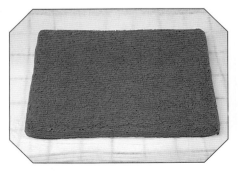

4 Dredge the paper with caster sugar. When baked, immediately turn out the sponge onto the paper, then remove the baking paper.

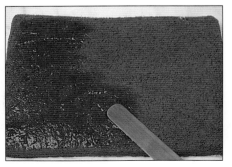

5 Leave to cool for a few minutes, spread preserves over the top. (For cream fillings, roll up the sponge, cool, unroll then fill.)

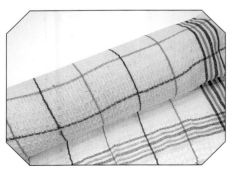

6 Immediately roll up the sponge and keep tightly covered with the damp cloth until cold. Then remove cloth and paper.

# BUTTERCREAM

## INGREDIENTS

115g butter, at room
 temperature (4oz)
170-225g icing sugar, sifted (6-8oz)
Few drops vanilla extract
1-2tbsp milk

This recipe can be flavoured and
coloured as desired.

NOTE: When making buttercream
use only fresh butter that is at a
temperature of 18-21°C (65-70°F).
Adding too much colouring to
buttercream can make it strong and
bitter so add a few drops at a time,
tasting between additions.

1 Beat the butter until light and
fluffy.

2 Beat in the icing sugar, a little at a
time, adding the vanilla extract and
sufficient milk to give a fairly firm
but spreading consistency.

# FUDGE ICING

## INGREDIENTS

200g icing sugar (7oz)
30g golden syrup (1oz)
1½tbsp milk
45g butter (1½oz)

The icing can be used in several ways: As a coating icing – pour over the cake as soon as the icing is
thick enough to coat the back of a spoon.
As a frosting or filling – allow the mixture to cool and beat briskly with a wooden spoon until like butter
cream.
For piping – when thick enough to hold its shape, put in a piping bag and use for decoration as desired.
This icing can be stored in a refrigerator or freezer and melted down again to a flowing consistency.
Coffee fudge frosting can be made by the addition of 10ml (2 tsps) coffee essence.
Chocolate fudge icing can be made by the addition of 20ml (2 heaped tsps) cocoa and 10ml (2 tsps) hot
water.

1 Sift the icing sugar into a bowl.
Then put remaining ingredients
into a small saucepan and stir over
low heat until the butter has
melted.

2 Bring to almost boiling then
immediately pour the mixture into
the icing sugar.

3 Stir until smooth. Follow the
suggestions for the various uses of
this fudge icing.

# SUGARPASTE

## INGREDIENTS

2tbsp cold water
1½ level tsp powdered gelatine
1½tbsp liquid glucose
2tsp glycerin
450g icing sugar, sifted (1lb)

Flavour sugarpaste to counteract sweetness by using peppermint, orange, vanilla etc.
Add a little vegetable fat or egg white if the paste is too dry.
Sugarpaste should be rolled out on an icing sugar or cornflour dusted surface. Icing sugar gives a matt finish while cornflour gives a satin finish.
Always warm sugarpaste slightly if cold before use.
The drying time for sugarpaste is approximately 24 hours but may vary according to moisture in the air.

  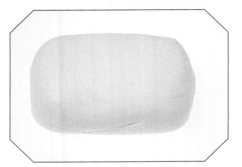

1 Pour the water into a saucepan and sprinkle on the powdered gelatine. Dissolve over low heat. Stir in the glucose and glycerin then remove from the heat.

2 Gradually add and stir in the icing sugar with a spoon, to avoid making a lumpy mixture. When unable to stir anymore icing sugar into mixture, turn out onto table.

3 Mix in the remaining icing sugar using fingers then knead until a pliable smooth paste is formed. Store in a sealed container for at least 24 hours or until required.

# MODELLING PASTE

## INGREDIENTS

255g icing sugar (9oz)
1 level tbsp gum tragacanth
1 level tsp liquid glucose

## STORAGE

Store in a refrigerator using a food-approved polythene bag in an airtight container. Always bring to room temperature before use.

  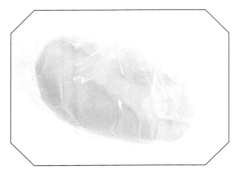

1 Thoroughly sift together the icing sugar and gum tragacanth into a mixing bowl.

2 Blend the glucose and water together then pour into the dry ingredients and mix well.

3 Knead the mixture by hand until a smooth and pliable paste is formed. To store see instructions above.

## ALBUMEN SOLUTION

### INGREDIENTS

15g pure albumen powder (½oz)
85g cold water (3oz)

## ROYAL ICING

### INGREDIENTS

100g fresh egg whites or
 albumen solution (3½oz)
450g icing sugar, sifted (1lb)

If using fresh egg whites,
separate 24 hours before use.

Royal icing should always have a
clean glossy appearance, good white
colour and a light texture.
When making royal icing, add the
icing sugar slowly and then beat well
to avoid a grainy texture.
Under-mixed royal icing has a creamy
look and should be beaten further.

### FOR SOFT CUTTING ROYAL ICING

For every 450g (1lb) ready-made
royal icing beat in the following
amounts of glycerin:

1tsp for bottom tier of three
 tiered cake.
2tsp for middle tiers.
3tsp for top tiers, single tiers
 and general piping.

Always make up sufficient coloured
icing as it will almost be impossible to
match the colour later.
Cover bowls of royal icing with a
clean, damp cloth to prevent drying
out.
Stipple royal icing using a clean
household sponge or palette knife.

**DO NOT ADD GLYCERIN WHEN MAKING
RUNOUTS, FIGURE PIPING, PIPED FLOWERS
AND LEAVES OR FINE LINE WORK.**

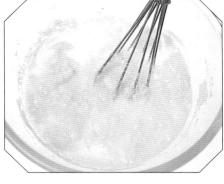

1 For albumen solution: Pour the
water into a bowl, then stir and
sprinkle in the albumen powder.
Whisk slowly to half-blend in. The
solution will go lumpy. Leave for
1 hour, stirring occasionally.

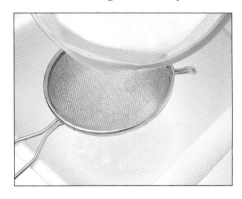

2 Pour the solution through a fine
sieve or muslin. It is now ready for
use. Store in a sealed container and
keep in a cool place until required.

1 For royal icing: Pour the egg
whites or albumen solution into a
bowl. Slowly mix in half the icing
sugar until dissolved.

2 Then slowly mix in the remaining
sugar. Run a spatula around the
inside of the bowl to ensure all the
ingredients are blended together.

3 Thoroughly beat mixture until light
and fluffy. Peaks should be formed
when the spoon or beater is lifted.
Clean down inside then cover
with a damp cloth until required.

**1** **To cover a round or square sponge cake:** Coat the cake-side and top with a thin layer of buttercream. Chill for 1 hour in the refrigerator.

**2** When chilled, roll out the sugarpaste and place over the cake, using the rolling pin.

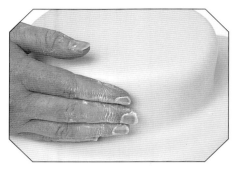

**3** Smooth the paste over the top, then down the side, using palm of hand. Trim around the cake-base or board edge. Leave until dry before decorating.

**1** **Covering a round or square fruit cake:** Fill-in any imperfections with almond paste. Brush boiling apricot purée over the cake-top and sides.

**2** Roll out almond paste, dusting with icing sugar and place over the cake, using the rolling pin. Then press firmly to the cake-top and sides using palm of hand to expel any trapped air. Leave to dry for 24

**3** Brush the almond paste with cooled boiled water. Roll out sugarpaste, dusting with icing sugar and place over the cake. Smooth to expel any trapped air. Trim paste and leave until dry before decorating.

## COLOURING SUGARPASTE

Add a very small amount of edible food colouring to the paste using a cocktail stick or skewer. Knead the paste thoroughly and then roll out to ensure there is no streaking.

Sufficient sugar paste should be made at one time as it is virtually impossible to match the colour later.

Protect coloured sugarpaste from strong light.

## MOTTLED SUGARPASTE

Mottled sugarpaste can be made by half mixing with the required colour before rolling out the paste.

## CRIMPING

Crimping must be carried out before sugarpaste is dry. Dip crimping tool into icing sugar. Push tool gently into paste before squeezing the crimper. Carefully release pressure and remove crimper.

To achieve best results, use even pressure on each crimp. The harder the crimp, the more defined the shape will be.

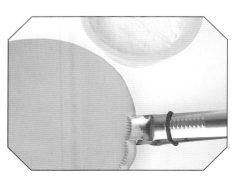

These steps are for covering cakes with almond paste ready for coating with royal icing.

*For coating cakes with royal icing see page 24.*
*For covering cakes with sugarpaste see page 22.*

**1** For a round cake: Roll out almond paste using icing or caster sugar for dusting. Brush top of cake with boiling apricot purée. Upturn cake onto the almond paste and then cut around as shown.

**2** Place cake on board. Roll out almond paste into strip that is long and wide enough to cover side of cake in one piece. Spread a thin layer of apricot purée over paste.

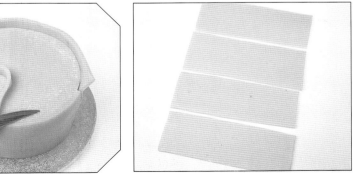

**3** Fix the almond paste to the side of the cake and trim off the surplus with a sharp knife. Leave to dry for 3 days before coating with royal icing.

**4** For a square cake: Roll out paste into half the thickness used on the cake top. Cut into 4 equal strips to fit the sides of a square cake. Spread apricot purée on the strips.

**5** Fix strips to the sides of the cake. Trim away any surplus cutting towards the centre using a sharp knife. Leave for 3 days before coating with royal icing.

# QUICK and EASY COATING

Coating with royal icing should ideally be carried out on a cake that has been covered in almond paste and allowed to dry thoroughly (three to four days). The smoother the almond paste, the better the royal icing.

The cake, carefully positioned on a board 7.5cm (3in) larger, should be placed on a turntable (see Equipment p.10).

If pale coloured icing is required, make the first coat white, the second a pale shade of the colour required, and the final coat the actual colour. When strong colours are used, the first coat should be half strength, the second three-quarter and the final coat full strength.

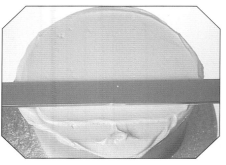

1 Spread royal icing over the cake-top with a stiff palette knife.

2 With a metal rule, smooth evenly over the top with a full forward and backward motion.

3 Bring the surplus icing down to cover the side, adding more as necessary.

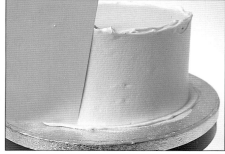

4 Using a scraper, smooth the side by rotating the turntable whilst keeping the scraper still. Then slide the scraper away.

5 Alternatively, use a serrated scraper on the side with an up and down motion to create the effect shown.

6 Remove the surplus icing from the cake-top. Leave to dry for 12 hours. Repeat twice more.

7 Spread royal icing around the cake board with a palette knife.

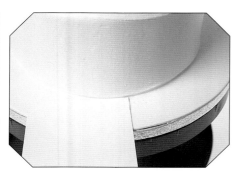

8 Smooth with a scraper whilst rotating the turntable. Leave to dry for 12 hours.

# BRUSH EMBROIDERY/PIPED SHAPES

## BRUSH EMBROIDERY

RECIPE: 3 tablespoons of royal icing mixed with ¼ teaspoon of clear piping gel.

 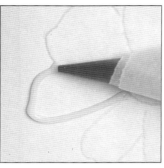 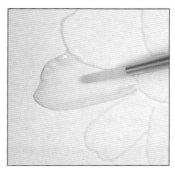 

**1** Trace or scribe a drawing onto a cake, covered with sugarpaste or royal icing, when dry.

**2** Using the recipe above, pipe a line onto one petal (No.2).

**3** Immediately brush the icing to the centre of the petal to achieve the feather like effect shown.

**4** Repeat steps 2 and 3 to complete all the petals and leaves. Then pipe-in the flower centres and stems (No.2).

## PIPED SHAPES

Use an upturned cake tin to practice on. Always pipe onto a dry surface. Piped work must always be dry before starting overpiping.

**Shell:** Place the piping tube against the surface and press. Continue pressing and start to lift the piping bag. With the piping bag slowly moving upwards, continue pressing until the size required is reached. Stop pressing, move the piping bag down to the surface and pull away to complete the shape.

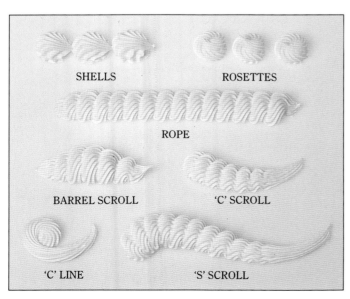

SHELLS      ROSETTES

ROPE

BARREL SCROLL      'C' SCROLL

'C' LINE      'S' SCROLL

**Rosette:** Holding the piping bag upright, move and press in a clockwise direction. On completion of one full turn, stop pressing and draw the piping bag away to complete the shape.

**Rope:** Holding the piping bag at a low angle, pipe a spring shape along the surface in a clockwise direction. Continue piping until length required, then stop. Pull the piping bag away to complete the shape.

**Barrel scroll:** Hold the piping bag at a low angle and start to press. Continue piping in a clockwise direction, increasing the size of the circle with each turn. Continue piping in clockwise direction but, from the centre, decrease the size of the circle with each turn. To complete the barrel scroll, stop piping and pull bag away in a half-turn.

**'C' scroll:** Pipe in a clockwise direction, increasing size. Continue piping, reducing size then form the tail using reduced pressure.

**'C' line:** Holding the piping bag at a slight angle, move and press in an anti-clockwise direction. Release the pressure whilst sliding the piping tube along the surface, to form a tail and complete the shape.

**'S' scroll:** Hold piping bag at a low angle and start to press. Continue piping in a clockwise direction, increasing the size of each circle to form the body. Continue piping, reducing the size of the circles from the centre. Continue piping and form the tail by reducing the pressure.

# SWEET PANDA

INGREDIENTS

20.5cm round sponge cake (8in)
 2 required
900g sugarpaste (2lb)
115g royal icing (4oz)
Assorted food colours

EQUIPMENT and DECORATIONS

28cm round cake board (11in)
Crimper
Blossom cutters
Piping tube No.1 and 2
Board edge ribbon

1 Sandwich the two sponge cakes together with filling of choice (jam, lemon or orange curd, flavoured buttercream etc).

2 Coat the cake with a thin layer of buttercream and place in a refrigerator to chill.

3 When chilled, place the cake onto the board and cover with sugarpaste. Then crimp around the edge as shown.

4 Using the template as a guide, cut out and fix a sugarpaste panda to the cake-top. Pipe the mouth with royal icing (No.2).

5 Cut out and fix a sugarpaste banner. Pipe inscription of choice with royal icing (No.1). Using a blossom cutter, cut out and fix sugarpaste blossoms.

6 Decorate the cake with more sugarpaste blossoms and then pipe the leaves with royal icing (No.1). Fix ribbon around the cake board edge.

# BUTTERFLY

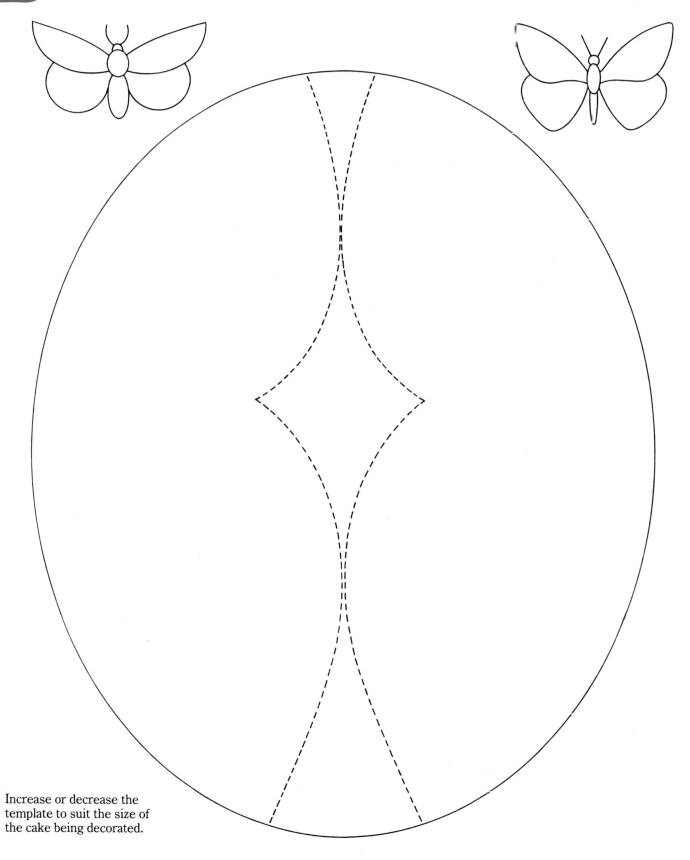

Increase or decrease the
template to suit the size of
the cake being decorated.

## INGREDIENTS

25.5cm oval sponge cake (10in)
Small swiss roll
450g sugarpaste (1lb)
225g buttercream (8oz)
Assorted food colours

## EQUIPMENT and DECORATIONS

35.5cm petal shaped cake board (14in)
Serrated scraper
Various shaped cutters
Crimper
Piping tube No.1
Candles and holders

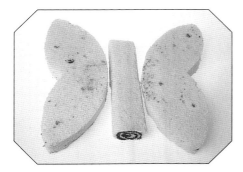

**1** Cover the board with sugarpaste and crimp the edge. Using the template as a guide, cut the sponge in half and trim to form butterfly wings.

**2** Trim the swiss rolls to body shape and cover with sugarpaste as shown. Cut and fix sugarpaste face pieces.

**3** Coat the wings with buttercream, using a serrated scraper. Place onto the board with the body, then decorate with sugarpaste cut-outs. Pipe inscription (No.1).

# PARTY BEARS

INGREDIENTS

25.5cm round sponge cake (10in)
 2 required
900g buttercream (2lb)
Coloured granulated sugar

EQUIPMENT and DECORATIONS

30.5cm round cake board (12in)
Serrated scraper
Piping tubes No.6 and 7

Small paint brush
Jelly diamonds
Birthday plaque

1 Layer sponge cakes together and coat with buttercream, using a serrated scraper for the side. Pipe rosettes around cake-base (No.7). Fix a jelly diamond onto each rosette.

2 Using template as guide, cut out a bear from centre of a card. Mark cake into 6 divisions. Place card over first mark and sprinkle on coloured granulated sugar.

3 Complete the cake-top with various coloured bears. Stipple the buttercream around the bears using a paint brush. Pipe shells around the cake-top edge (No.6). Fix plaque to the cake-top.

# KING TROLL

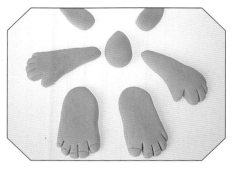

1 Fix the sponges together and trim as shown. Sprinkle a few drops of green food colouring onto desiccated coconut and mix well.

2 Spread a thin layer of buttercream over the cake board then sprinkle with coconut. Spread buttercream over the sponge and sprinkle with coconut, coloured brown.

3 Make and fix the various parts, using sugarpaste. Make and fix sugarpaste eyes. Place the fork as shown in main picture.

Sponge cake baked in a 1.2 Lt
  pudding basin (2pt)
Sponge cake baked in a 600ml
  pudding basin (1pt)
225g buttercream (8oz)

225g sugarpaste (8oz)
Desiccated coconut
Brown, green and black food
  colours

28cm round cake board (11in)
Decorative fork
Board edge ribbon

# TOY BOX

## INGREDIENTS

15cm square sponge cake (6in)
 4 required
1.5k sugarpaste (3lb)
170g royal icing (6oz)
Assorted food colours

## EQUIPMENT and DECORATIONS

25.5cm square cake board (10in)
Decorative board covering
15cm square cake card (6in)
Piping tubes No.1 and 2
Candles and holders
Board edge ribbon

**1** Cover the board with decorative paper. Layer sponges together and then cover with two colours of sugarpaste. Fix the sponge to the cake card then to the board.

**2** Using the templates on page 36 as a guide, cut out sugarpaste teddy bears and umbrellas. Pipe the lines shown, with royal icing (No.1).

**3** When dry, fix the cut-outs to the cake-sides. Make and fix sugarpaste corners. Pipe shells as shown (No.2).

**4** Make a sugarpaste rabbit head and bear.

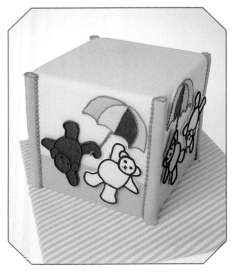

**5** Fix to the cake-top. Then make and fix a sugarpaste clown and sticks. Decorate the board with sugarpaste cut-outs and piped inscriptions (No.1).

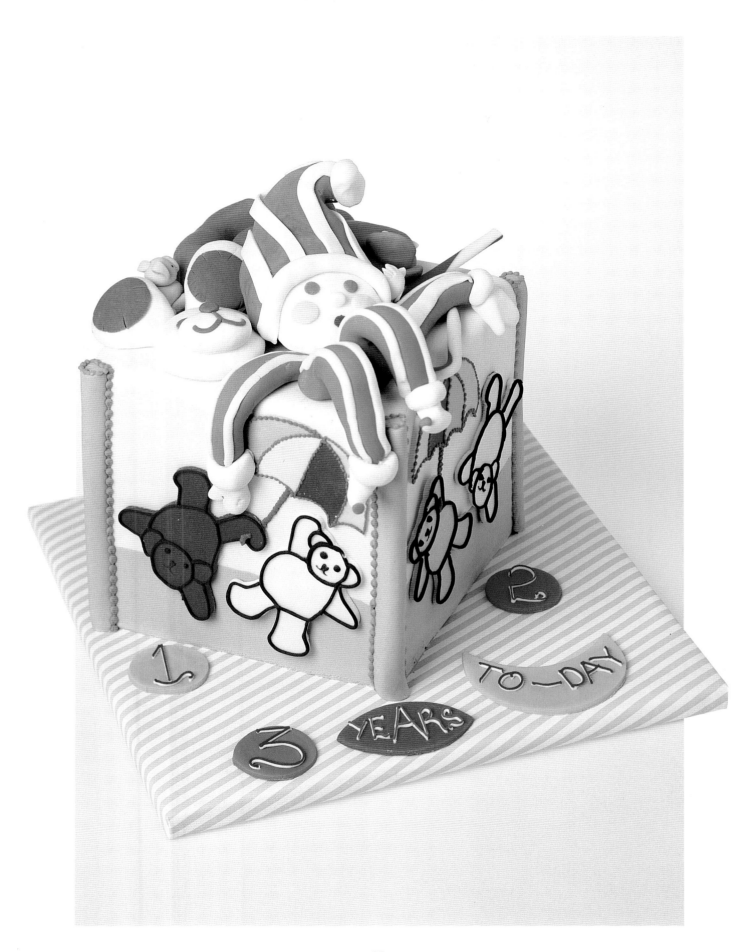

# SPRING TIME

INGREDIENTS

25.5cm round sponge cake (10in)
 2 required
680g buttercream (1½lb)
Green and apricot food colours

EQUIPMENT and DECORATIONS

30.5cm round cake board (12in)
Serrated scraper
Paint brush
Rice paper
Dusting powder

Piping tubes No.7 and 59
Non-stick paper
Jelly diamonds
Green coloured coconut
Birthday motto

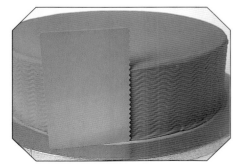

**1** Coat the sponge with buttercream using a serrated scraper for the sides. Place in the refrigerator for 1 hour to chill. Sprinkle a few drops of food colour onto desiccated coconut and mix well.

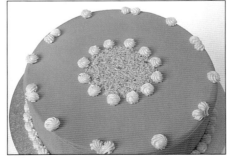

**2** Pipe buttercream flowers (see p.154) onto non-stick paper and chill in the refrigerator. Cut butterfly wings from rice paper and colour with dusting powder. Make as many as required.

**3** Sprinkle coloured coconut onto the cake-top centre. Then pipe rosettes and shells as shown around the cake-top edge and base (No.7). Fix the flowers and butterflies as required.

# CLOWNING AROUND

## INGREDIENTS

Sponge cake baked in a 1.2Lt
 pudding basin (2pt)
Sponge cake baked in a 600ml
 pudding basin (1pt)
2 miniature swiss rolls
1.5k sugarpaste (3lb)
115g royal icing (4oz)
Assorted food colours

## EQUIPMENT and DECORATIONS

35.5cm round cake board (14in)
Rainbow sugar crystals
Cocktail stick
Piping tube No.2
Jelly diamonds
Miniature flowerpot
Party hat
Plastic flowers

38

1 Coat the board with royal icing and immediately sprinkle rainbow sugar crystals over the surface. Leave to dry.

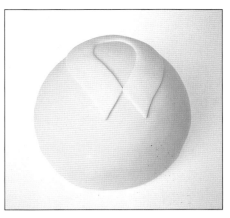

2 **For the body:** Cover the large sponge with sugarpaste. Then cut out and fix a sugarpaste collar.

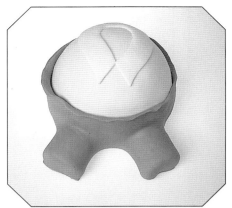

3 Fix the swiss rolls to the body for the legs. Then roll out sugarpaste and fix and fold around the body and legs to form trousers.

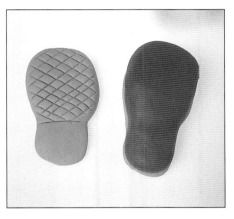

4 Make two pairs of sugarpaste shoes as shown. Mark soles of shoes with a cocktail stick.

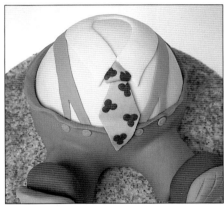

5 Fix the shoes to the legs. Then cut out and fix sugarpaste braces and tie. Decorate with cut-out flower shapes and buttons.

6 **For the head:** Cover the small sponge with sugarpaste. Cut out and fix sugarpaste eyes and mouth. Then mould and fix nose. Pipe the lines shown with royal icing (No.2).

7 Cut out a strip of sugarpaste. Then cut into long strands to form the hair. Fix around the head.

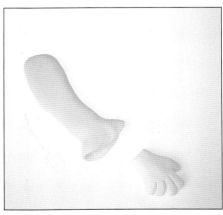

8 Mould a pair of sugarpaste arms and hands and fix to the sides of the body.

9 Fix the miniature flowerpot into position. Then sprinkle in jelly diamonds as shown.

# CROCODILE FUN

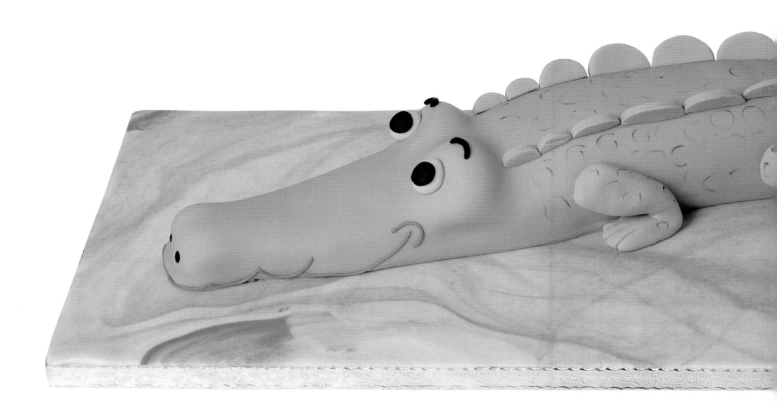

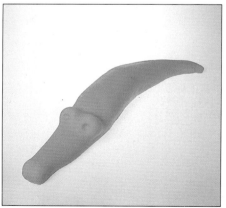

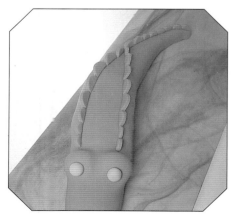

1 Slice one swiss roll diagonally. Place end to end then fix half of the other swiss roll between. Cover with a thin layer of buttercream and chill in a refrigerator.

2 When chilled, fix two sugarpaste humps onto the head for the eyes, then cover all with sugarpaste. Cover the board with mottled sugarpaste.

3 Cut and fix semi-circles of sugarpaste for the back bones. Make and fix the eyes.

2 large swiss rolls
1.5k sugarpaste (3lb)
115g buttercream (4oz)
115g royal icing (4oz)
Assorted food colours

25.5 x 66cm oblong cake
 board (10 x 26in)
Round cutters
Fine paint brush
Piping tube No.2

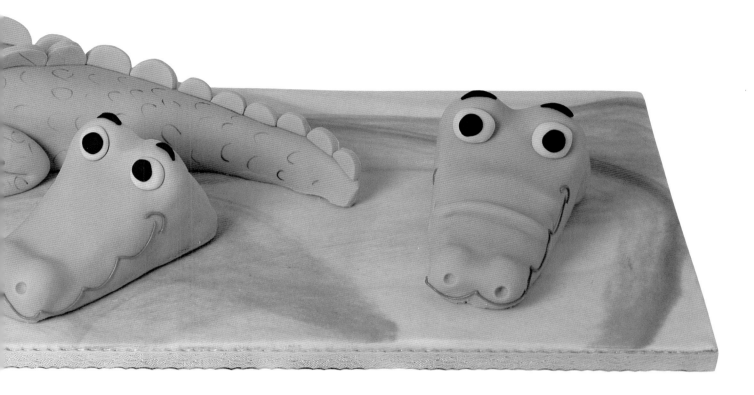

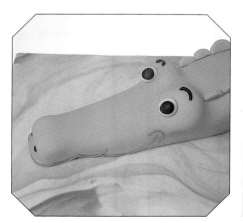

4 Make and fix sugarpaste pupils. Pipe eyebrows and mouth, with royal icing (No.2).

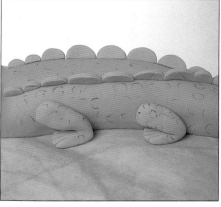

5 Paint the lines on the crocodile to form the pattern shown.

6 Cut the remaining swiss roll piece in half and make into crocodile heads as shown.

# CASH REGISTER

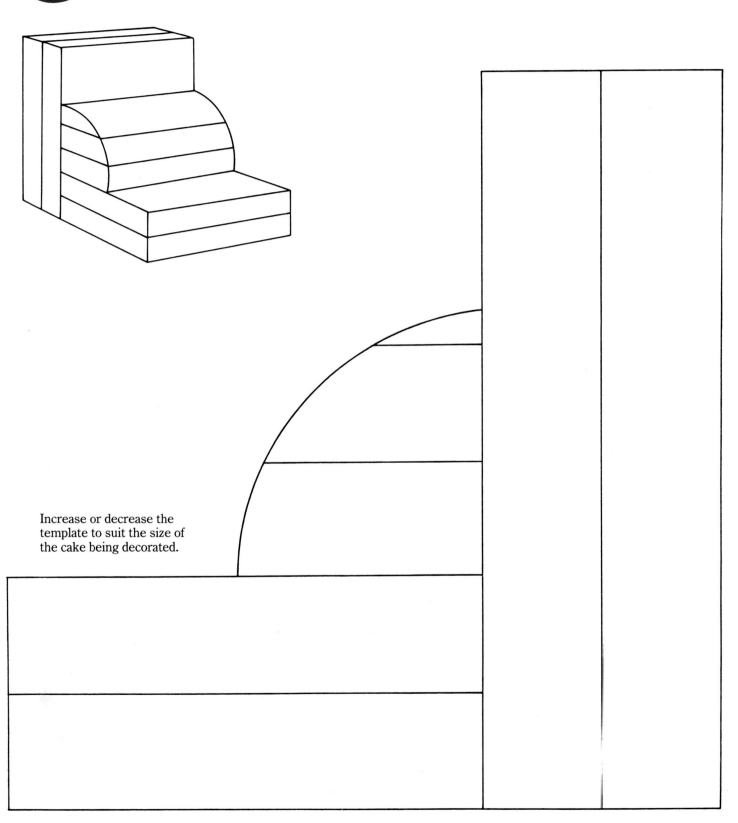

Increase or decrease the
template to suit the size of
the cake being decorated.

## INGREDIENTS

20.5cm square sponge cake
 (8in) 4 required
1.5k sugarpaste (3lb)
225g royal icing (8oz)
Assorted food colours

## EQUIPMENT and DECORATIONS

35.5 x 25.5cm oblong cake
 board (14 x 10in)
Decorative board covering
Cake card
Food grater
Piping tubes No.1, 2 and 43
18mm round cutter (¾in)
Chocolate coins
Candles and holders

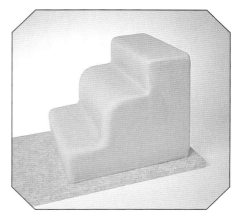

**1** Cover the board with decorative paper. Layer and cut the sponges to form the till shape. Fix to the cake card, then cover with sugarpaste.

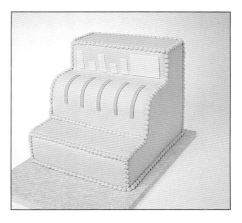

**2** Cut out a piece of sugarpaste for the drawer top and mark with the grater. Fix to the cake. Cut out and fix the other sugarpaste pieces as shown. Pipe shells with royal icing around the cake (No.43).

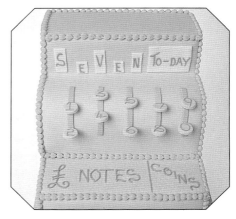

**3** Cut out and fix sugarpaste buttons. Pipe figures and inscription as required (No.2 and 1).

20.5cm square sponge cake
 (8in) 2 required
1.5k sugarpaste (3lb)
225g royal icing (8oz)
Demerara sugar
Assorted food colours

28cm square cake board (11in)
Fine paint brush
Motto
Board edge ribbon

1 Coat the board with royal icing and immediately sprinkle on demerara sugar to form sand effect. Make 2 small sandcastles in the same manner.

2 Layer the sponges together, place upright and cover with sugarpaste. Cut and fix strips of sugarpaste as shown.

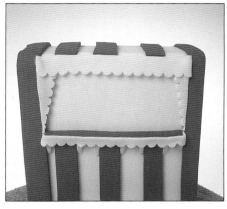

3 Cut out sugarpaste pieces and fix to the front to form stage surround.

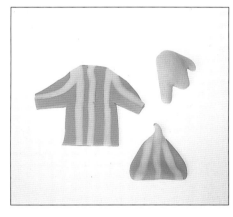

4 Make the various parts of Punch, using sugarpaste, as shown.

5 Fix the pieces together and decorate as required. Fix to the cake-side.

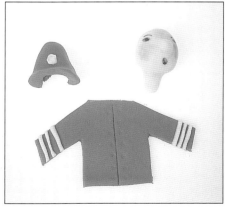

6 Make the various parts of the policeman with sugarpaste.

7 Fix the pieces together and decorate as required. Fix to the cake-side. Make and fix various sugarpaste beach items.

# BIRTHDAY SALUTE

INGREDIENTS

15cm round sponge cake (6in)
 2 required
20.5cm square sponge cake (8in)
 2 required

115g royal icing (4oz)
2k sugarpaste (4lb)
Assorted food colours

EQUIPMENT and DECORATIONS

35.5 cm square cake board (14in)
Round cutters
Cotton wool or candy floss
Dowelling
Board edge ribbon

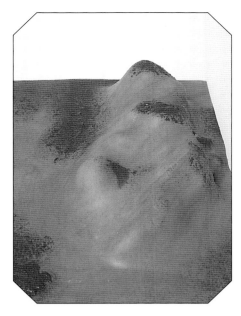

1 Using the template as a guide, cut the round sponges to an oval shape. Place the off-cuts onto the board and cover with sugarpaste as shown.

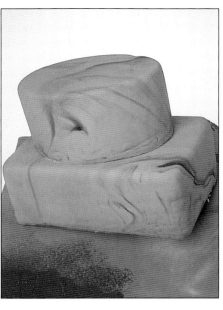

2 Using the template as a guide, cut pieces off the square sponges to form tank body and tracks. Cover the top and body with mottled sugarpaste.

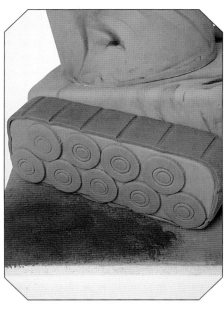

3 Cover the tracks with sugarpaste as shown and fix to the tank.

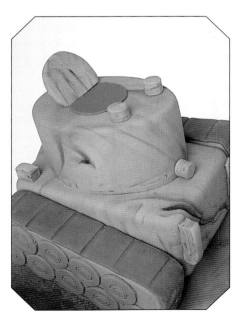

4 Make and fix various sugarpaste parts to the tank.

5 Make and fix a sugarpaste gun barrel supported with dowelling. Fix cotton wool or candy floss to the end.

6 Mould sugarpaste into two balls and wings for each duck, as shown.

7 Fix the pieces together, then make and fix feet and beak.

8 Make and fix a sugarpaste hat. Pipe the eyes with royal icing (No.1).

9 Make as many ducks as required and fix to the tank in various positions.

Increase or decrease the template to suit the size of the cake being decorated.

Increase or decrease the template to suit the size of the cake being decorated.

# MacDONALDS FARM

## INGREDIENTS

20.5cm square sponge cake (8in)
 2 required
1.5k sugarpaste (3lb)
225g royal icing (8oz)
Assorted food colours

## EQUIPMENT and DECORATIONS

30.5cm square cake board (12in)
Coarse sieve
Piping tube No.1
Paint brush
Ruler
Motto
Board edge ribbon

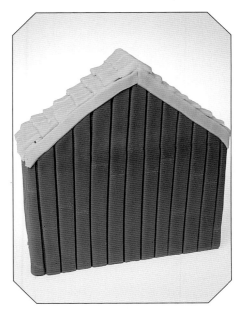

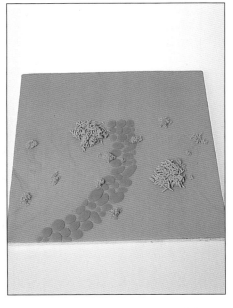

1 Cut the sponges to barn shape, layer, then cover with sugarpaste. Press a ruler into the sugarpaste to form planks. Cut and fix sugarpaste pieces to form the roof.

2 Stipple the board with royal icing and decorate with sugarpaste to form ground and path.

3 Cut and fix sugarpaste barn doors. Brush with colouring as shown.

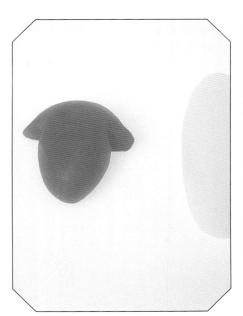

4 **To make sheep:** mould the head and then the body, using sugarpaste.

5 Fix the pieces together then place onto non-stick paper. Brush with royal icing to form the coat, then pipe the eyes as shown (No.1). Leave until dry.

6 **To make pigs:** mould the body, head and nose with sugarpaste in the proportions shown.

50

7 Fix the pieces together then make and fix feet, ears and tail. Pipe the eyes with royal icing (No.1).

8 To make chickens: mould the body, head and wings with sugarpaste.

9 Fix the pieces together then make and fix the crown. Pipe the eyes with royal icing (No.1).

10 To make cow heads: mould the basic shape with sugarpaste. Make and fix the horns, then a nose ring. Pipe the hair and eyes with royal icing (No.1).

11 Fix the barn to the decorated board. Push sugarpaste through a wire sieve, to form straw, and fix to the barn and ground as shown.

12 Fix the animals as required. Fix the motto to the front of the barn. Fix ribbon around the board edge.

# PIERROT

INGREDIENTS

20.5cm round sponge cake (8in)
 2 required
450g buttercream (1lb)
Assorted food colours

EQUIPMENT and DECORATIONS

28cm round cake board (11in)
20.5cm round cake card (8in)
Piping tubes No.3 and 44
Small petal tube

Cling film
Ribbon bow
Sugar hearts

1 Using the template as a guide outline Pierrot with buttercream (No.3) onto cling film placed over the cake card.

2 Fill-in Pierrot with various colours of buttercream. Place into refrigerator to chill.

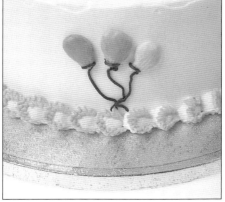

3 Layer, then coat the sponge with buttercream. Pipe shells around the cake-base (No.44). Pipe a scalloped line onto each shell using the small petal tube. Pipe balloons and strings (No.3).

4 When chilled, upturn Pierrot onto cling film, then transfer to the cake-top. Pipe shells around the cake-top edge (No.44). Pipe a dot between each shell (No.3). Fix sugar hearts and ribbon bow.

# BIRTHDAY BUNNY

## INGREDIENTS

Sponge cake baked in a 1.2Lt
 pudding basin (2pt)
Sponge cake baked in a 600ml
 pudding basin (1pt)
450g buttercream (1lb)
225g sugarpaste (8oz)
Assorted food colours

## EQUIFMENT and DECORATIONS

30.5cm round cake board (12in)
Rice paper
Piping tube No.1
Decorative flowers
Board edge ribbon

1 Stipple the board with buttercream. Then stipple the sponges with buttercream and place onto the board, as shown.

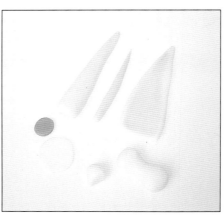

2 Mould the various parts of the rabbit, using sugarpaste.

3 Fix the pieces to the rabbit. Then cut and fix rice paper whiskers. Make and decorate a sugarpaste carrot. Pipe inscription (No.1). Decorate the board with flowers.

# LUCKY BLACK CAT

## INGREDIENTS

Sponge cake baked in a 1.2Lt
  pudding basin (2pt)
Sponge cake baked in a 600ml
  pudding basin (1pt)
340g buttercream (12oz)
Desiccated coconut
170g sugarpaste (6oz)
Assorted food colours

## EQUIPMENT and DECORATIONS

25.5cm round cake board (10in)
Spaghetti strands
Plastic motto
Board edge ribbon

1 Fix the sponges together then cover with buttercream, using a fork to make fur effect. Stipple buttercream onto the board and sprinkle with coloured desiccated coconut.

2 Cut out and fix sugarpaste eyes, nose, ears and tail.

3 Cut out and fix a sugarpaste collar, bow and tongue. Insert spaghetti strands as shown.

# NEW ARRIVAL

 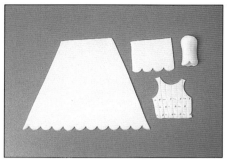 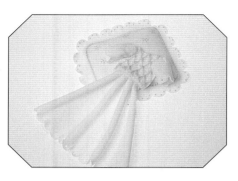

1 Cover the cake and board with sugarpaste. Fix Christening ribbon around the cake-side. Make and fix sugarpaste frills around the cake-top edge and base. Emboss the edges as shown.

2 Using the templates as a guide, cut out and mark sugarpaste as shown. Cover with polythene. Then make the pillow.

3 Fold and fix the dress pieces together onto the pillow. Then decorate with piped smocking (No.1). Fix to the cake-top. Pipe inscription of choice (No.1) and decorate with flowers and ribbon bow.

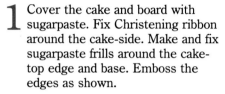

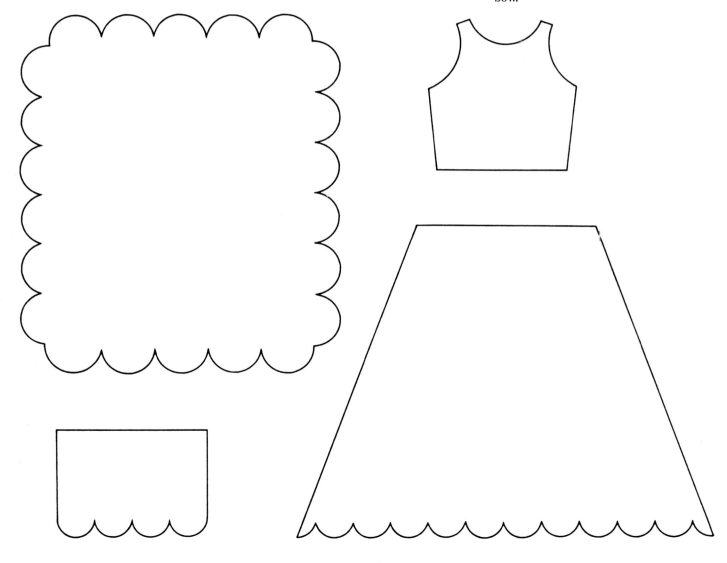

20.5cm round fruit cake (8in)
680g almond paste (1½lb)
1.5k sugarpaste (3lb)
115g royal icing (4oz)
French pink food colour

28cm round cake board (11in)
Embosser
Tweezers
Piping tube No.1
Crimped cutter

Ribbon bow
Blossoms
Christening ribbon
Board edge ribbon

# MY CHRISTENING

## INGREDIENTS

20.5cm round sponge cake
 (8in) 2 required
900g sugarpaste (2lb)
115g modelling paste (4oz)
Blue food colour

## EQUIPMENT and DECORATIONS

28cm round cake board (11in)
Crimper
Piping tube No.1
Miniature heart shaped cutter
Embosser
Table tennis ball
Christening ribbon
Flowers
Ribbon bows
Board edge ribbon

1 Cover the cake and board with sugarpaste. Crimp around the cake-top edge, side and board as shown.

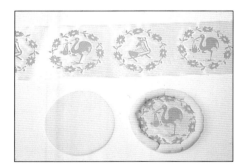

2 Cut the ribbon into circles. Make and emboss circles of sugarpaste and fix to the ribbon, then fix around the cake-side.

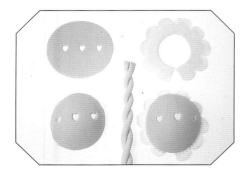

3 Fix and emboss a sugarpaste roll around the cake-base. Make rattle pieces with modelling paste, using tennis ball as a mould. Fix to cake-top and decorate as required.

# BABY JOE

## INGREDIENTS

20.5cm square fruit cake (8in)
900g almond paste (2lb)
900g royal icing (2lb)
Lemon and blue food colours

## EQUIPMENT and DECORATIONS

25.5cm square cake board (10in)
Patterned side scraper
Piping tubes No.1, 2 and 44

Narrow ribbon
Ribbon bows
Flowers

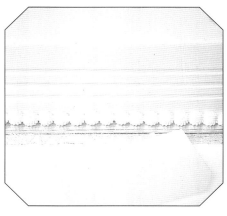 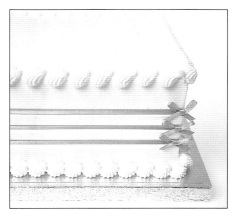 

1 Coat the cake with royal icing, using the patterned scraper for the cake-side. When dry, pipe shells around the cake-base (No.44).

2 Fix ribbon into the grooves around the cake-side. Fix bows to the front corner. Pipe shells around the cake-top edge (No.44). Pipe a dot between each shell (No.2).

3 Pipe the outline of a stork onto the cake-top (No.2). Pipe inscription of choice (No.1). Decorate the cake with flowers.

# SWEET DREAMS

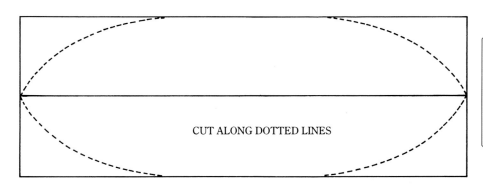

CUT ALONG DOTTED LINES

Increase or decrease the template to suit the size of the cake being decorated.

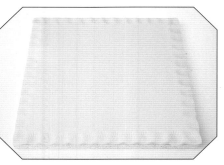

**1** Cover the board with sugarpaste and immediately press a modelling tool around the border to form the pattern shown.

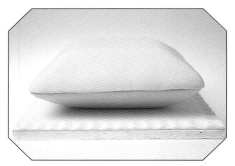

**2** Using the template as a guide, trim the cake sides then cover the top with sugarpaste, upturn and then cover with sugarpaste to seal the cake as shown.

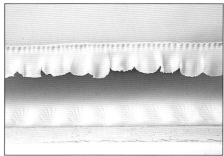

**3** Cut out and fix a fluted strip of sugarpaste around the edge of the cake. Press with the end of a paint brush to form the pattern.

**4** Cut out and fix sugarpaste hearts.

**5** Make and fix a sugarpaste pillow. Pipe the decoration with royal icing (No.1). Place a plastic baby against the pillow.

**6** Make and fix a sugarpaste shawl. Decorate with royal icing (No.1).

**7** Pipe and decorate the name (No.1). Fix a ribbon bow to each corner of the cake.

20.5cm square sponge cake (8in)
 2 required
1.5k sugarpaste (3lb)
115g royal icing (4oz)
Pink food colour

25.5cm square cake board (10in)
Small heart shaped cutter
Piping tube No.1.
Paint brush
Small crimper

Modelling tool
Plastic baby
Ribbon bows
Board edge ribbon

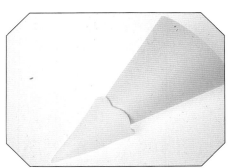

1 Cover the cake and board with sugarpaste. Using the template as a guide, cut out modelling paste and place over a paper cone to dry. Approximately 16 pieces required.

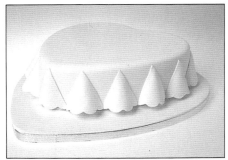

2 Fix narrow ribbon around the cake-base. When dry, fix the pieces to the cake-side with royal icing, slightly raised off the board.

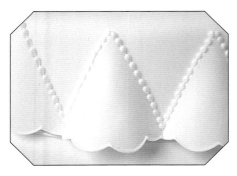

3 Pipe shells along each side of the cone shapes and then a line along the bottom edge (No.2).

## INGREDIENTS

23 cm heart shaped fruit
  cake (9in)
900g almond paste (2lb)
900g sugarpaste (2lb)
225g modelling paste (8oz)
225g royal icing (8oz)
Silver dusting powder
Spearmint green food colour

## EQUIPMENT and DECORATIONS

30.5cm heart shaped cake
  board (12in)
Non-stick paper
Scalloped shaped cutter
Plastic doyley
Piping tubes No.1 and 2
Large candle
Narrow ribbon
Board edge ribbon

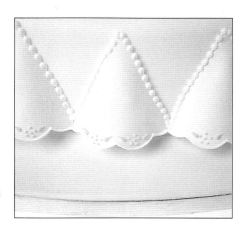

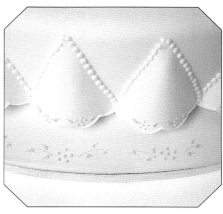

4 Pipe floral pattern on each cone as shown (No.1).

5 Pipe the floral pattern shown around the cake board (No.1).

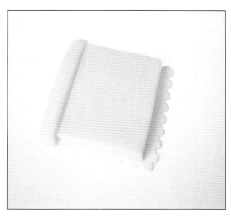

6 Cut 2 pieces of modelling paste for book cover.

7 Cut and shape the inside pages with sugarpaste and fix as shown.

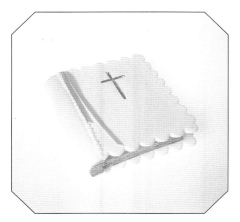

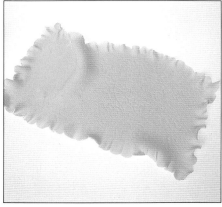

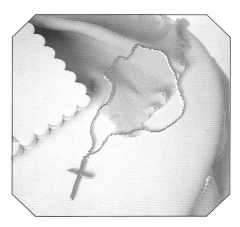

8 Fix the front cover, then decorate the book as required.

9 Cut out and frill a sugarpaste shawl, pressing with doyley to make pattern. Fix the shawl and book to the cake-top.

10 Pipe a chain and cross (No.1). Paint with silver dusting powder moistened with pure alcohol. Pipe inscription of choice (No.1).

# TIMOTHY

## INGREDIENTS

2 large swiss rolls
680g sugarpaste (1½lb)
115g royal icing (4oz)
Assorted food colours

## EQUIPMENT and DECORATIONS

35.5 x 30.5cm oval cake
 board (14 x 12in)
Decorative board covering
Cake card

Piping tube No.2
Candle
Board edge ribbon

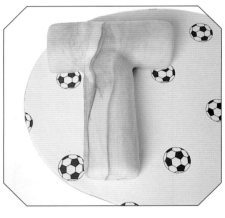

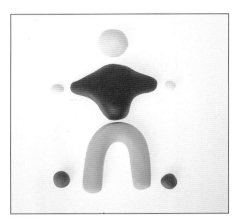

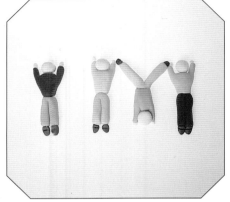

1 Fix the decorative covering to the board. Fix the sponges together then cover with mottle coloured sugarpaste. Cut card to fit between the sponge and the board then fix.

2 Mould various shapes with sugarpaste for the figures.

3 Fix the pieces together. Make as many figures as required to spell the chosen name and others climbing over the cake. Pipe the line and words (No.2).

# TWINS DELIGHT

## INGREDIENTS

20.5cm square sponge cake (8in)
 2 required
450g buttercream (1lb)
450g chocolate flavoured
 cake covering (1lb)
1 teaspoon glycerin
115g royal icing (4oz)
Green food colour

## EQUIPMENT and DECORATIONS

30.5cm square cake board (12in)
Heat-proof bowl
Saucepan
Non-stick paper
Fluted cutters
Piping tubes No.1 and 44
Jelly diamonds
Icing sugar for dusting

## TO MAKE PIPING CHOCOLATE

Break 340g of the chocolate (12oz) into pieces and place into a heat-proof bowl over a saucepan of simmering water. Stir until melted. Remove from heat and stir in the glycerin, a little at a time, until a soft piping consistency is reached. Keep the mixture warm during use.

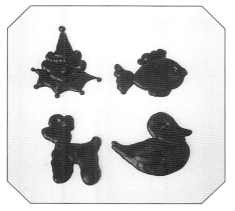

1 Using the templates as a guide, pipe piping chocolate onto non-stick paper and leave until set.

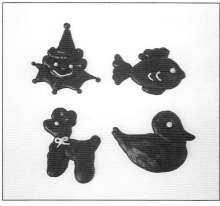

2 When set, decorate the shapes with royal icing (No.1).

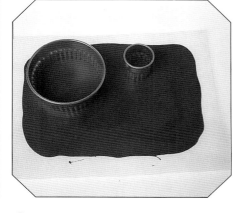

3 Melt remaining 115g (4oz) of chocolate in a bowl over simmering water. When melted spread onto non-stick paper and leave until just set, then cut out crimped circles as required. Leave until set hard.

4 Layer and coat the sponges with buttercream. Place into refrigerator to chill slightly.

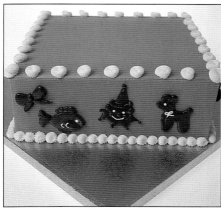

5 Pipe shells around the cake-base and rosettes around the cake-top edge as shown, with buttercream (No.44). Fix figures around the cake-sides.

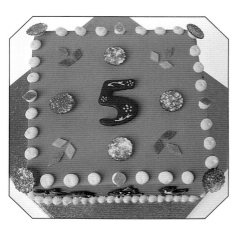

6 Decorate the cake-top with chocolate cut-out circles, numeral and jelly diamonds. Pipe inscriptions onto large circles and fix to the board.

# THE GOOSE GIRL

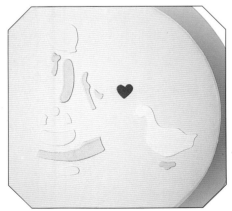

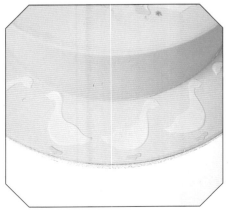

1 Coat cake and board with royal icing. Leave until dry. Trace templates onto card, cut out with a scalpel knife. Place onto the cake-top, spread over with royal icing then pull card away.

2 Pipe the decoration as shown (No.1). Paint in the ground with food colourings.

3 Repeat step 1 for the birds around the cake board.

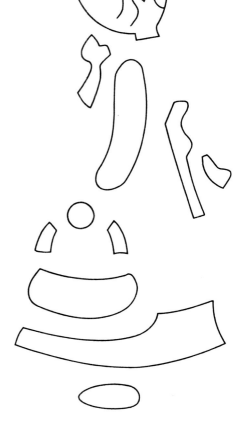

INGREDIENTS

20.5cm round fruit cake (8in)
680g almond paste (1½lb)
900g royal icing (2lb)
Assorted dusting powers
Assorted food colours


EQUIPMENT and DECORATIONS

30.5cm round cake board (12in)
Card for stencil
Scalpel knife
Piping tubes No.1, 2, 43 and 57
Fine paint brush
Narrow ribbon
Board edge ribbon

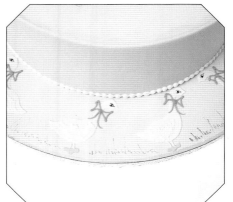

4 Pipe shells around the cake-base (No.2). Then decorate the birds (No.1).

5 Pipe curved rope lines around the cake-top edge (No.43). Overpipe the rope lines (No.2).

6 Pipe a wavy line beside the No.43 line (No.57) then overpipe the No.2 line (No.1). Pipe inscription of choice (No.1). and fix ribbons as required.

# AMERICAN FOOTBALL

## INGREDIENTS

Sponge cake baked in a 1.2Lt
 pudding basin (2pt)
680g sugarpaste (1½lb)
115g royal icing (4oz)
Assorted food colours

## EQUIPMENT and DECORATIONS

28cm round cake board (11in)
Piping tube No.2
Coarse cloth
Football players
Board edge ribbon

1 Cover the board with sugarpaste
and mark with a coarse cloth.
Cover the sponge with sugarpaste
as shown.

2 Cut out and fix sugarpaste pieces
to the helmet as shown.

3 Cut out and fix the face and bars
with sugarpaste. Pipe inscription of
choice with royal icing (No.2). Fix
figures as required.

# WEIGHT LIFTING

## INGREDIENTS

20.5cm round sponge cake (8in)
680g sugarpaste (1½lb)
115g royal icing (4oz)
Black and red food colours

## EQUIPMENT and DECORATIONS

25.5cm square cake board (10in)
Piping tube No.1
Bone tool or paint brush

1 Trim the side of a round sponge to form a weight shape. Cover with sugarpaste and make rings, using a bone tool or end of a paint brush.

2 Make and fix sugarpaste bar and nut.

3 Make and decorate small sugarpaste weights around the cake board. Make and fix a sugarpaste plaque.

INGREDIENTS

20.5 cm round sponge cake (8in)
 3 required
1.5k sugarpaste (3lb)
225g royal icing (8oz)
Assorted food colours

EQUIPMENT and DECORATIONS

28 cm round cake board (11in)
Blossom cutters
Piping tubes No.1 and 42
Narrow ribbons
Board edge ribbon

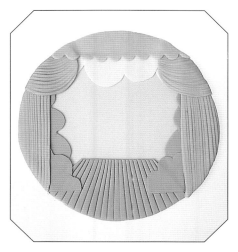

1 Cover the cake with sugarpaste, then the board. Cut out and fix sugarpaste stage and scenery to the cake-top. Pipe shells around the edge with royal icing (No.42).

2 Using a blossom cutter, cut out and fix sugarpaste flowers around the cake-base. Mould sugarpaste parts for the small pigs around the cake-side.

3 Fix to the cake-side then pipe the eyes with royal icing (No.1).

4 Cut and fix tutus and shoes. Pipe the pupils (No.1).

5 Make and decorate the main pig for the cake-top as shown.

6 Link the side pigs together with strips of sugarpaste. Cut out and fix flowers.

73

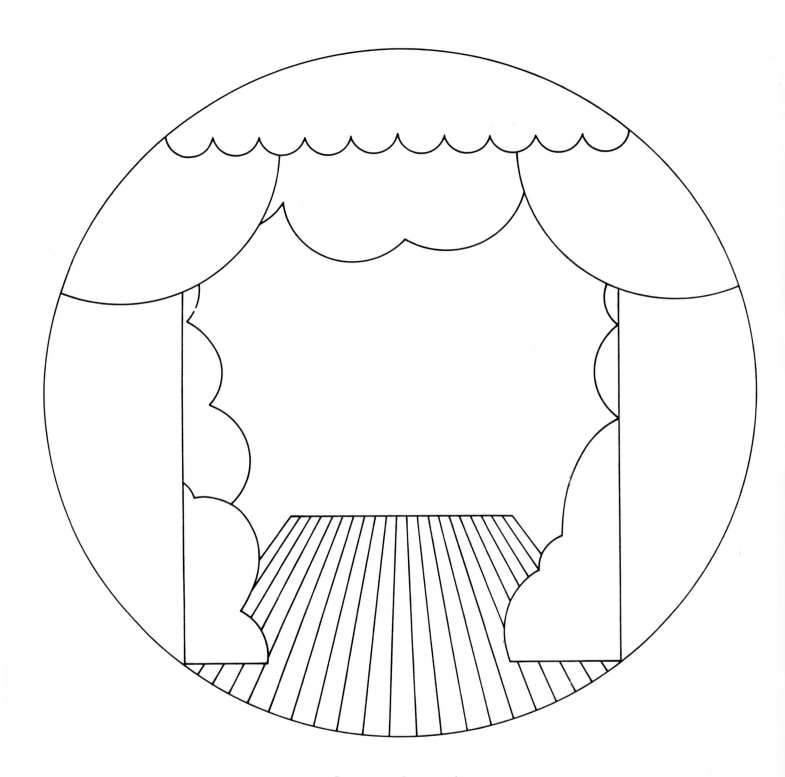

Increase or decrease the
template to suit the size of
the cake being decorated.

25.5cm round sponge cake (10in)
 2 required
2k sugarpaste (4lb)
115g royal icing (4oz)
Assorted food colours

35.5cm round cake board (14in)
Piping tube No.1.
Spaghetti strands
Green card

1 Cut an irregular piece from one sponge then cover both pieces with mottled sugarpaste.

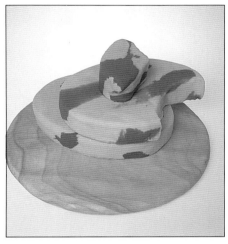

2 Cover the remaining sponge with mottled sugarpaste. Cover the board with mottled sugarpaste then fix the sponges as shown.

3 Make the head of a monkey in the sequence shown.

4 Make the various parts for the body.

5 Fix the pieces together as shown. Make as many as required.

6 Make a sugarpaste panda as shown.

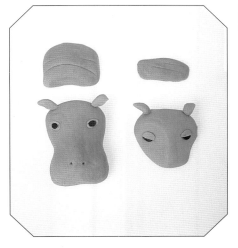

7 Make a sugarpaste male and female hippopotamus head and back as shown.

8 Make a selection of sugarpaste ducks.

9 Make sugarpaste trees, stiffened with spaghetti strands. Cut and fix leaves from card. Fix to the cake as required, then fix a monkey as shown.

10 Fix the hippopotamus and ducks to the board. Pipe the ripples shown with royal icing (No.1).

11 Fix another monkey and sugarpaste bananas. Fix the panda and sugarpaste bamboo shoots.

12 Make sugarpaste snakes and curl around candles. Make and fix as many as required.

# VIDEO GAMES

INGREDIENTS

20.5cm square sponge cake (8in)
3 required
1.5k sugarpaste (3lb)
115g royal icing (4oz)
Assorted food colours

EQUIPMENT and DECORATIONS

40.5cm square cake board (16in)
Decorative board covering
Cake cards

Piping tube No.1
Knife
Paint brush

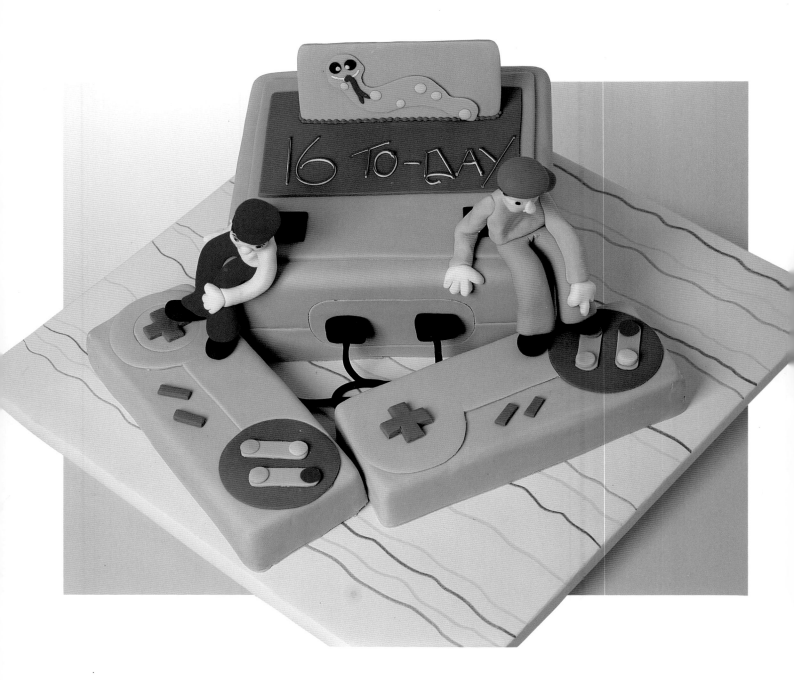

78

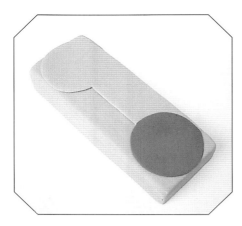

1 Cut one sponge in half and cover both pieces with sugarpaste. Cut and fix sugarpaste pieces as shown.

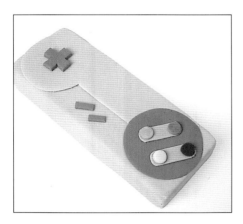

2 Cut out and fix sugarpaste buttons.

3 Layer the two remaining sponges and cover with sugarpaste. Cut out and fix a square of sugarpaste onto the cake-top. Mark the sides, using the back of a knife.

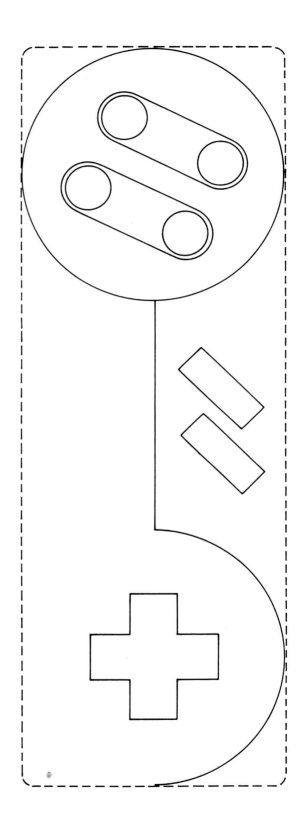

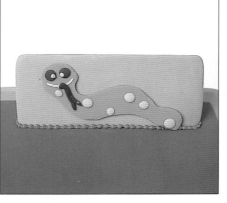

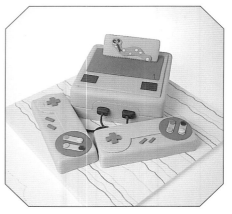

4 Cut out and fix sugarpaste pieces as shown.

5 Make and fix a sugarpaste screen. Decorate with a snake. Pipe shells with royal icing (No.1) along the cake-base.

6 Place the cakes on cake cards then fix the cakes onto the board. Link together with sugarpaste wires.

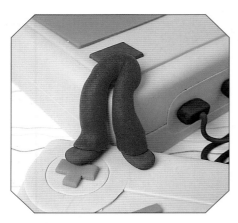

7 Mould sugarpaste legs and shoes, then fix as shown.

8 Mould and fix the body and arms.

9 Mould and fix head. Paint in eyes and hair. Mould and fix a hat. Repeat steps 7 to 9 for the second figure. Pipe inscription of choice (No.1).

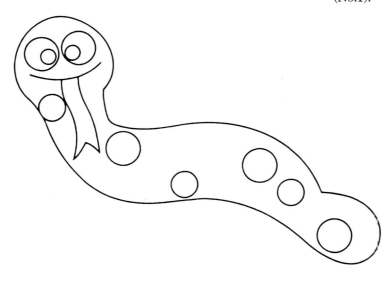

# SEA LIFE

INGREDIENTS

25.5 x 18cm oblong shaped
  sponge cake (10 x 7in)
  2 required
1.25k sugarpaste (2½lb)
170g royal icing (6oz)
Assorted food colours

EQUIPMENT and DECORATIONS

35.5cm square cake board (14in)
Coarse sieve
Fish shaped cutter
Birthday motto
Flowers
Board edge ribbon

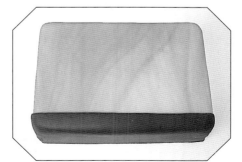

1 Layer the sponges together. Then cover with mottled sugarpaste. Cut out and fix sugarpaste to the front-side to form the tank, as shown.

2 Roughly coat the board with royal icing. Then place tank in position. Cut out and fix sugarpaste frame and fish.

3 Cut out and fix sugarpaste sea bed and seaweed. Then make and fix selection of sea shells and creatures for the cake board and sea bed.

# PENGUIN PLAYTIME

## INGREDIENTS

25.5 cm round sponge cake (10in)
 2 required
1.5k sugarpaste (3lb)
225g royal icing (8oz)
Meringue pieces
Assorted food colours

## EQUIPMENT and DECORATIONS

33 cm round cake board (13in)
Piping tube No.2
Board edge ribbon

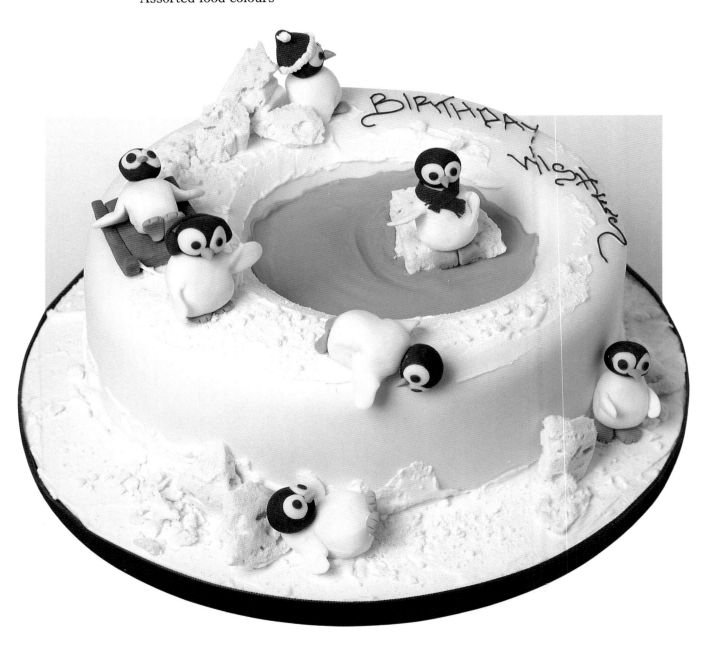

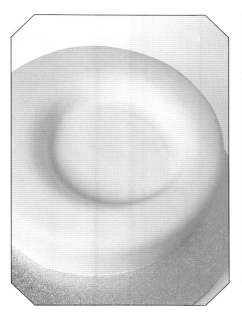

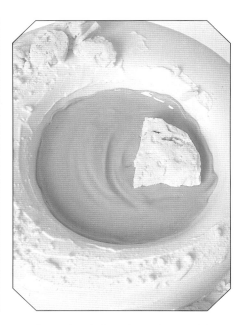

1 Cut out a hole, off centre, from one sponge then layer onto the remaining sponge Cover with sugarpaste.

2 Fix broken meringue pieces around the cake and board, then stipple with a little royal icing.

3 Spread a little softened royal icing into the cake-top centre. Fix a piece of meringue as shown.

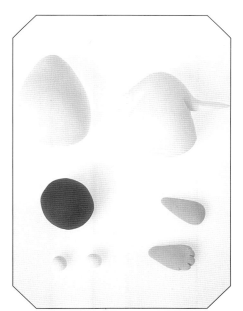

4 Mould and cut the various sugarpaste parts for a penguin.

5 Fix the parts together and decorate as required.

6 Repeat step 5 to make as many penguins as required. Fix the penguins to the cake and board. Pipe inscription of choice (No.2).

# WHEEL OF FORTUNE

## INGREDIENTS

30.5cm square fruit cake (12in)
2.5k almond paste (5lb)
2k sugarpaste (4lb)

225g royal icing (8oz)
Assorted food colours

## EQUIPMENT and DECORATIONS

35.5cm square cake board (14in)
Piping tube No.43

1 Using the template as a guide, mark the cake-top as shown.

2 Cut out and fix various colours of sugarpaste for the wheel, dice and markers.

3 Pipe shells around the cake-base with royal icing (No.43).

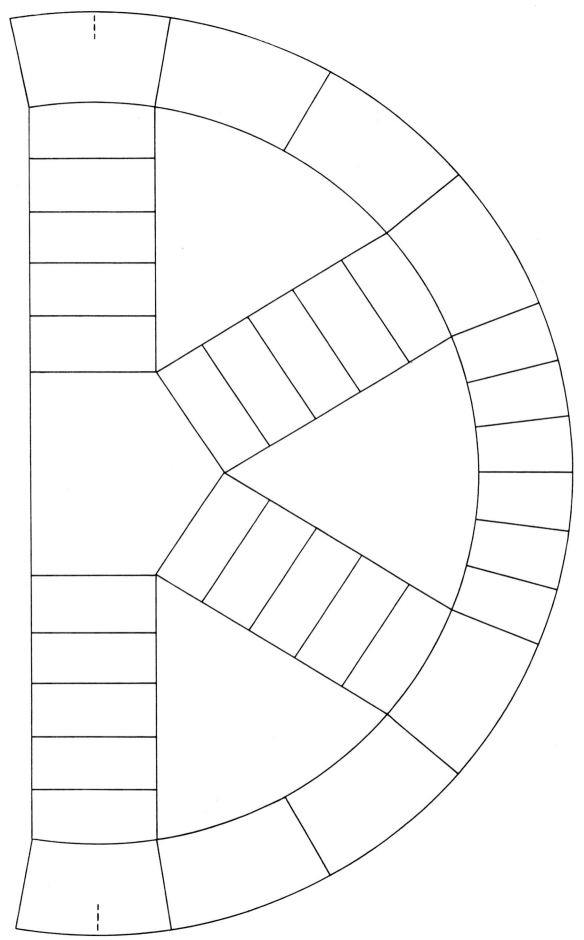

20.5cm square fruit cake (8in)
900g almond paste (2lb)
1.75k sugarpaste (3½lb)
115g royal icing (4oz)
Assorted food colours

25.5cm square cake board (10in)
20.5cm square cake card (8in)
Sieve
Paint brush

Non-stick polythene
Piping tube No.42
Board edge ribbon

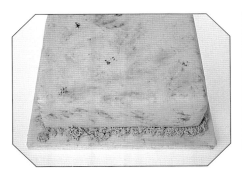

1 Cover the cake and board with sugarpaste. Brush colouring over the paste to form the ground. Sieve a little sugarpaste and fix around the cake-base.

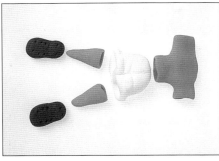

2 Mould the various sugarpaste parts for a player's clothes and boots.

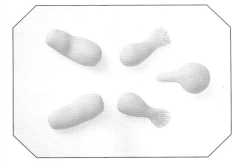

3 Immediately mould sugarpaste parts for the player's body.

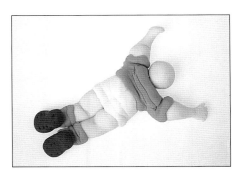

4 Fix the pieces, slightly squeezing together to form wrinkles as shown.

5 Rest the player on non-stick polythene to give movement then colour as shown. Make as many full and part players as required.

6 Fix the part players in a circle onto the cake-top.

7 Pile full players on top.

8 Cut out and colour various sugarpaste faces.

9 Cover the card with sugarpaste then fix on the faces to form the crowd. Fix the card to the back of the cake. Pipe shells along the top edge (No.42).

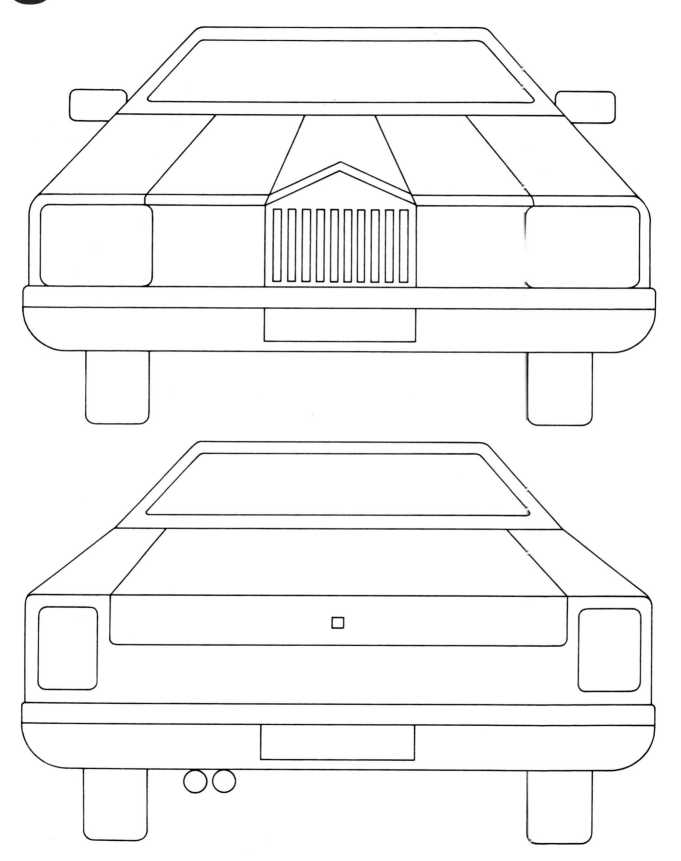

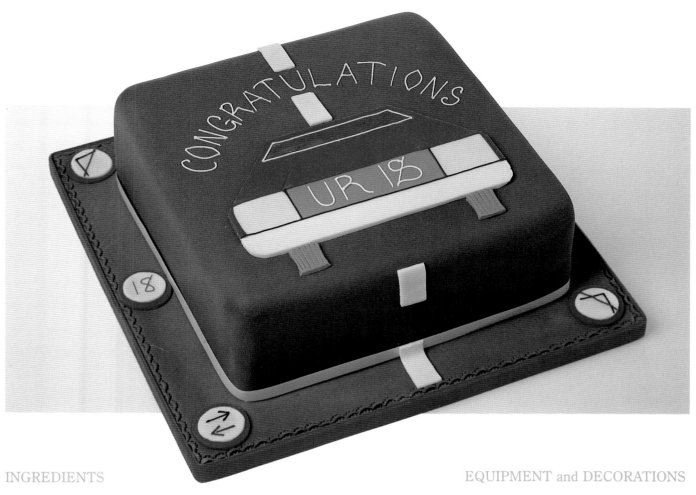

## INGREDIENTS

20.5cm square fruit cake (8in)
900g almond paste (2lb)
1.25k sugarpaste (2½lb)
115g royal icing (4oz)
Assorted food colours

## EQUIPMENT and DECORATIONS

28cm square cake board (11in)
Piping tube No.1
Round cutters
Narrow ribbon
Board edge ribbon

1 Cover the cake and board with sugarpaste. Cut and fix sugarpaste road lines. Fix a ribbon around the cake-base.

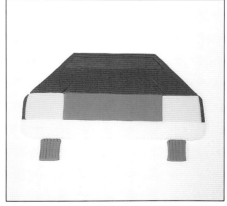

2 Cut out the car, front or back, from sugarpaste and leave until dry. Then fix to the cake-top.

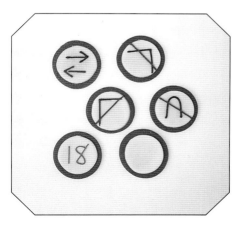

3 Cut out sugarpaste road signs and decorate with royal icing (No.1). Pipe inscription of choice (No.1).

# CHAMPAGNE SPARKLE

## INGREDIENTS

20.5 cm square sponge cake (8in)
 2 required
1.5k sugarpaste (3lb)
115g royal icing (4oz)
1 teaspoon of piping gel
Assorted food colours

## EQUIPMENT and DECORATIONS

40.5 cm round cake board (16in)
Paint brush
Cube sugar
Motifs and flowers
Board edge ribbon

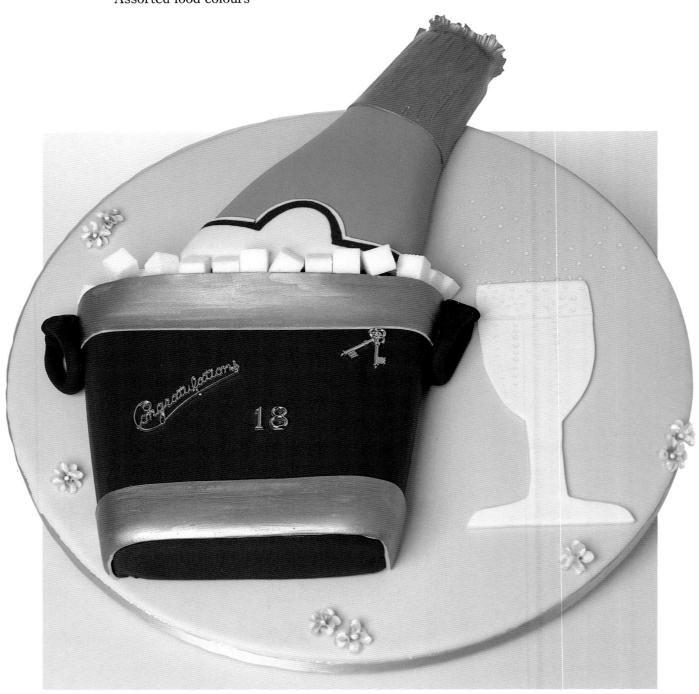

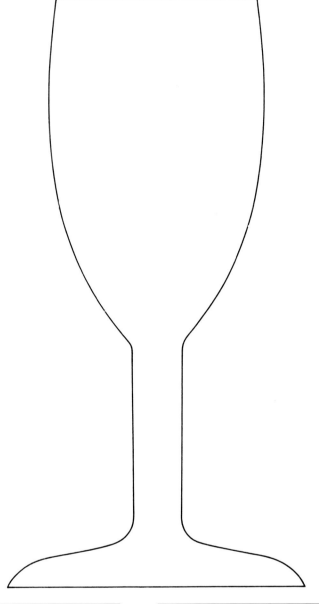

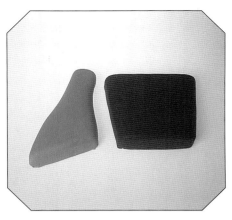

1 Using the templates as a guide trim the two sponges to form the bucket and portion of bottle. Cover with sugarpaste.

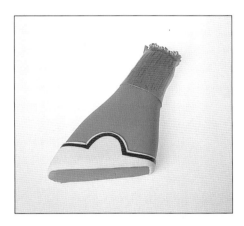

2 Cut out and fix a sugarpaste label and top. Brush with food colours as shown.

3 Cut and fix two strips of sugarpaste to the bucket. Brush with food colour. Make and fix sugarpaste handles.

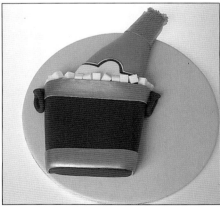

4 Cover the board with sugarpaste, then fix the bucket and bottle as shown. Fix sugar cubes to the rim.

5 Cut out and fix a sugarpaste glass. Then pipe piping gel to form bubbles. Decorate with appropriate flowers and motifs.

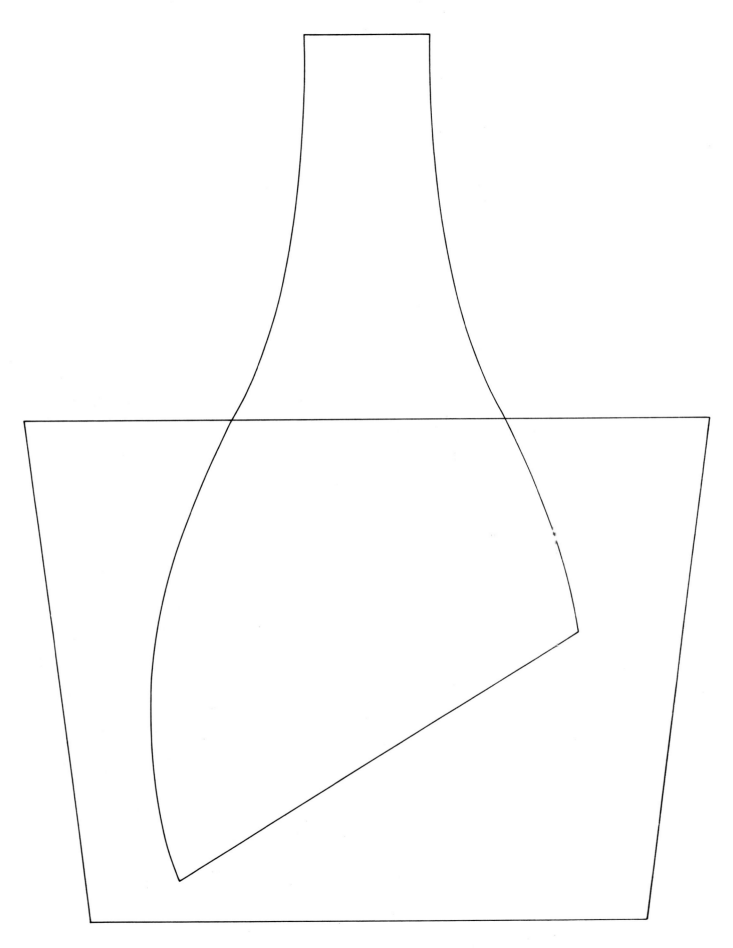

# TWENTY ONE YEARS

## INGREDIENTS

20.5cm square fruit cake (8in)
1.25k almond paste (2½lb)
1.25k sugarpaste (2½lb)
340g modelling paste (12oz)
115g royal icing (4oz)
Assorted food colours

## EQUIPMENT and DECORATIONS

35.5cm x 25.5cm oblong shaped
 cake board (14 x 10in)
Piping tubes No.1 and 2
Crimper
Fine paint brush

Modelling tools
Dowling
Assorted numerals and favours
Board edge ribbon

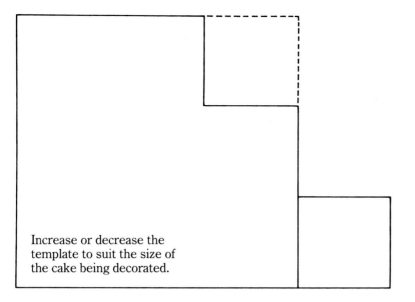

Increase or decrease the template to suit the size of the cake being decorated.

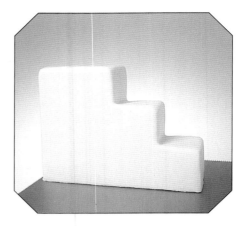

1 Cut a square from one corner of the cake. Place the cakes upright onto the board, fix together and cover with sugarpaste.

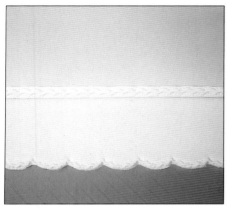

2 Cut out and fix fluted strips of sugarpaste around the cake as shown. Crimp the edge. Roll out and fix a band of sugarpaste to the cake-base and crimp.

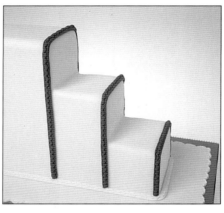

3 Roll out and fix bands of sugarpaste over the cake and crimp.

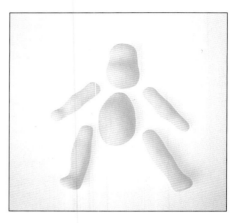

4 To make the baby: Mould the body, head, arms and legs from modelling paste.

5 Make a potty, then fix the baby pieces together and decorate as shown. Fix to the board.

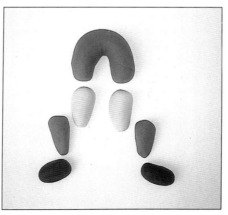

6 To make the young boy: Mould the trousers, knees, socks and shoes from modelling paste.

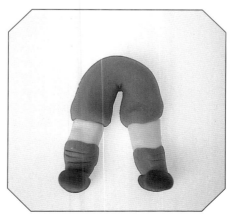

7 Fix, then slightly squash the pieces together to create the crinkle effect shown.

8 Mould the body pieces as shown.

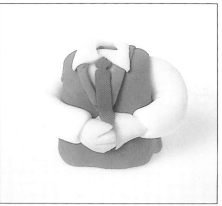

9 Fix the pieces together then cut and fix a tie.

10 Fix in a sitting position onto the cake, then make and fix the head and hat.

11 To make the teenager: Mould the various parts of the body from modelling paste.

12 Fix together onto the cake in the position shown. Make and fix a hat and glass.

13 To make the man: Mould the various parts shown from modelling paste.

14 Fix the pieces to the cake-top in the position shown.

15 Make and fix the head and hands. Cut and fix collar, cuffs and tie.

16 Curl narrow strips of modelling paste around dowling, leave to dry then fix to cake. Decorate cake with numerals and favours. Pipe inscription of choice with royal icing (No.2 and 1).

# COUCH POTATO

INGREDIENTS

20.5cm square sponge cake (8in)
1.25k sugarpaste (2½lb)
115g royal icing (4oz)
Assorted food colours

EQUIPMENT and DECORATIONS

35.5 x 25.5cm oblong cake
 board (14 x 10in)
Cake card
Decorative board covering

Cocktail stick
Fine paint brush
Crimper
Black food pen

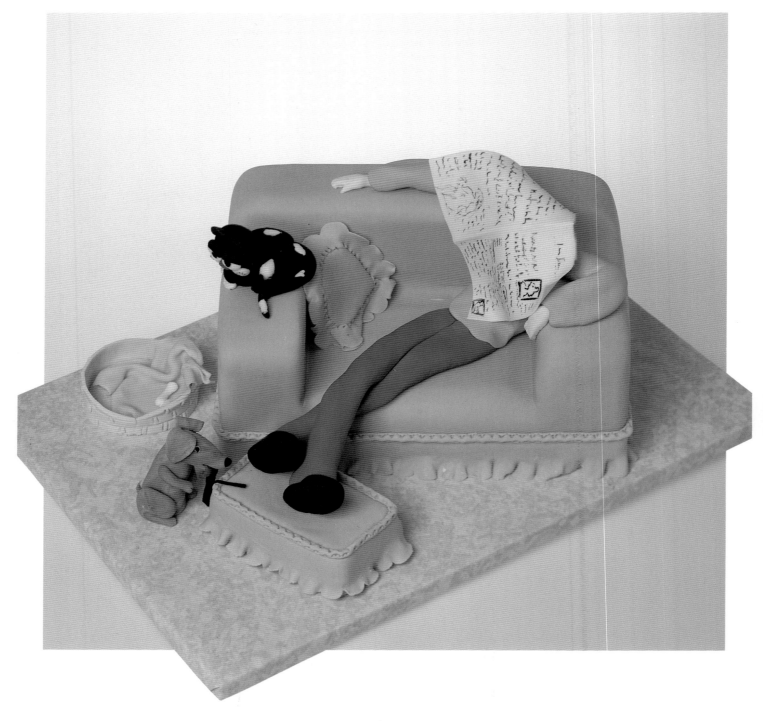

96

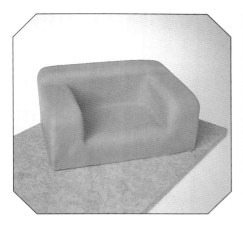

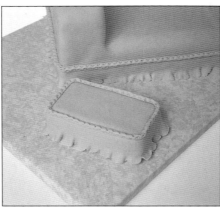

1 Cover the board with decorative covering. Using the template as a guide, cut sponge where indicated, then trim and fix together. Cover with sugarpaste. Fix to cake card then board.

2 Using the trimmings, cut and cover with sugarpaste to form a foot cushion. Fix to cake card. Cut and fix a sugarpaste frill around each base.

3 Make all the remaining steps with sugarpaste. Mould a long roll, fold in half and fix to the couch to form the legs. Make and fix slippers.

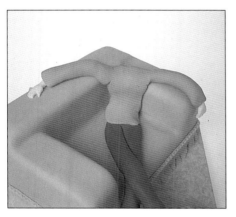

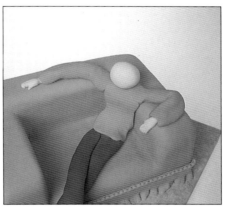

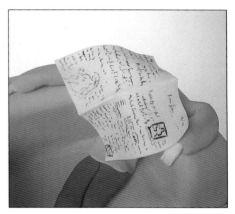

4 Mould and fix body and arms. Then make and fix the hands.

5 Roll out and fix the basic head shape.

6 Roll out and cut a thin piece of sugarpaste then write print effect with food pen. Fix as shown.

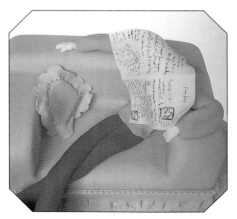

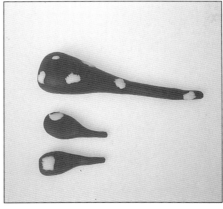

7 Make and fix a small cushion.

8 To make the cat: Mould the body and tail, then two back legs as shown.

9 Fix the back legs to the body then make and fix two front legs and paws.

97

10 Mould sugarpaste into a ball for the head. Cut and fix two semi-circles for the eyes.

11 Make and fix cheeks, nose, ears and pupils as shown.

12 Fix the head to the body and curve the tail as required. Fix to the couch as shown in the main picture.

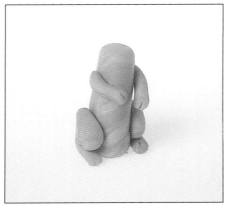

13 **To make the dog:** Mould the body, large back legs and small front legs as shown.

14 Fix the pieces together in an upright position.

15 Make the head and fix eyes, nose and tongue. Make the two large ears.

16 Fix the head to the body, then fix the ears. Make and fix a dog lead. Fix the dog to the board.

17 **To make the basket:** Cut out a circle and then a strip of sugarpaste for the side. Mark as shown, using a ruler or cocktail stick.

18 Fix the pieces together, then make and fix a sugarpaste blanket. Fix the basket to the board.

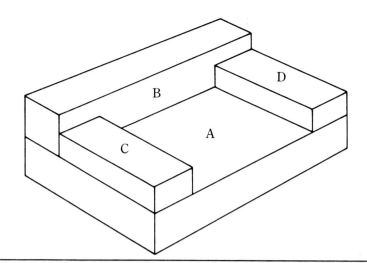

B

C          D

A

Increase the template to
match the size of the
cake being used.

# FISHERMAN'S HAT

1 Fix decorative paper to board. Fix sponge to cake card and lightly coat sponge with buttercream. Then roll out and fix a ring of sugarpaste to the cake-top edge.

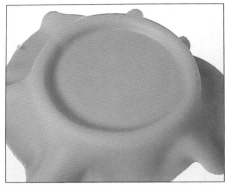

2 Cut out a large piece of sugarpaste and cover the whole sponge. Then press with a wide paint brush around inside edge of ring to form the hat crown.

3 Immediately cut the edge of the hat in an even circle. Then crimp the edge as shown.

4 Place the hat onto the cake board and shape the brim, supporting with tissue paper until dry.

5 Cover the small sponge with two colours of sugarpaste to form the fisherman's tackle box.

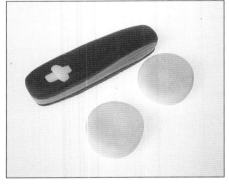

6 Make a Swiss penknife and small circular boxes from sugarpaste.

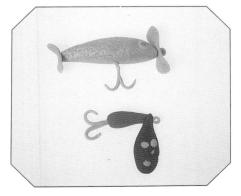

7 Make a selection of lures and sugarpaste flies.

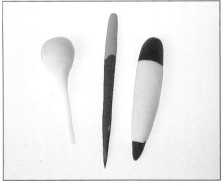

8 Make a selection of sugarpaste floats.

9 Cut silk leaves into strips to form feathers and fix to side of hat. Pipe inscription of choice onto tackle box with royal icing (No.1).

20.5cm round sponge cake (8in)
15 x 10cm oblong sponge
 (6 x 4in)
1.5k sugarpaste (3lb)
115g royal icing (4oz)
Assorted food colours

40.5 x 35.5cm oblong cake
 board (16 x 14in)
Cake card
Decorative board covering
Fine paint brush
Wide paint brush

Tissue paper
Crimper
Silk leaves
2.5cm round cutter (1in)
Piping tube No.1
Board edge ribbon

# LITTLE MONSTER

## INGREDIENTS

Sponge cake baked in a 1.2Lt
  pudding basin (2pt)
Sponge cake baked in a 600ml
  pudding basin (1pt)
1.25k sugarpaste (2½lb)
225g royal icing (8oz)
Assorted food colours

## EQUIPMENT and DECORATIONS

33cm round cake board (13in)
Piping tube No.2
Board edge ribbon

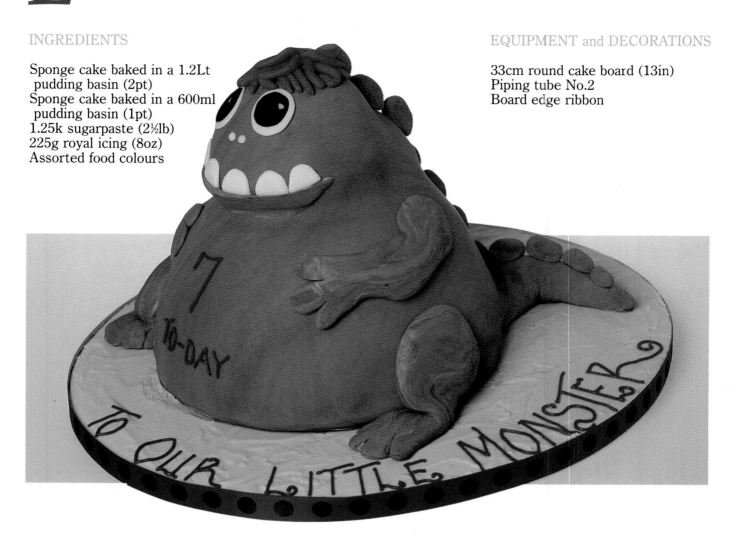

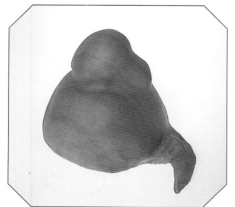

1 Fix the sponges together. Fix a lump of sugarpaste to the back of the neck then cover the whole sponge with sugarpaste. Make and fix a sugarpaste tail.

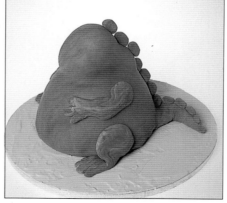

2 Fix the monster to the board. Stipple royal icing around the edge then make and fix sugarpaste arms, legs and back bones.

3 Cut out and fix sugarpaste mouth, teeth, eyes, nose and hair. Pipe inscription of choice with royal icing (No.2).

# SNOOKER CASE

1 Cover the board with sugarpaste and mark with the coarse cloth. Cut sponges in half, stack and layer together. Cut and fix sugarpaste top, then sides (slightly higher).

2 Cut and fix sugarpaste box liner and divider. Make the lid from the card and sugarpaste. Pipe inscription with royal icing (No.2). Leave to dry.

3 Make and place sugarpaste cues and chalk. Fix the box onto the board. Fix the lid to the box. Pipe shells around the lid (No.43). Make and fix sugarpaste balls.

## INGREDIENTS

20.5cm square sponge cake (8in)
 2 required
1.5k sugarpaste (3lb)
115g royal icing (4oz)
Assorted food colours

## EQUIPMENT and DECORATIONS

35.5 x 40.5cm cake board (14 x 16in)
10 x 40.5cm cake card (4 x 16in)
Piece of coarse mesh
Piping tubes No.2 and 43
Board edge ribbon

# SPARKY

## INGREDIENTS

20.5 x 25.5cm sponge cake
 (8 x 10in) 2 required
2k sugarpaste (4lb)
Assorted food colours

## EQUIPMENT and DECORATIONS

35.5cm square cake board (14in)
Piping tube No.1
Novelty cake candles

1 Cut and shape a sponge to shape shown, cover with sugarpaste and place onto a cake board.

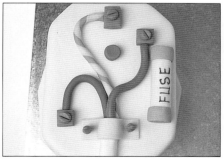

2 Make and fix sugarpaste wire, fuse and fixings.

3 Make and then pipe inscription onto a sugarpaste flash shaped plaque (No.1).

# BALL & CHAIN

INGREDIENTS

Sponge cake baked in a 600ml
 pudding basin (1pt) 2 required
680g sugarpaste (1½lb)
Black food colour

EQUIPMENT and DECORATIONS

28cm oval petal shaped cake
 board (11in)
Small cake card
Decorative board covering

Piping tubes No.1 and 2
Assorted flowers
Board edge ribbon

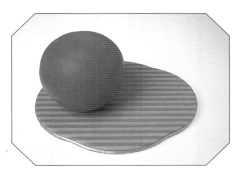

1 Cover the board with decorative
covering. Fix the 2 sponges
together and trim to form the ball.
Cover with sugarpaste and fix to
the cake card then the board.

2 Make rings of sugarpaste to form a
chain.

3 Make a sugarpaste band, fix to the
board then fix the chain as shown.
Pipe inscription of choice with
royal icing (No.2 and 1). Decorate
as required.

# THEATRE BUFF

INGREDIENTS

20.5cm square fruit cake (8in)
900g almond paste (2lb)
1.75k sugarpaste (3½lb)
225g modelling paste (8oz)
Blue and red food colours

EQUIPMENT and DECORATIONS

25.5cm square cake board (10in)
Black food pen
Crimper
Embosser
Board edge ribbon

1 Cover the cake and board with sugarpaste. Twist and fix sugarpaste strips to the cake-base.

2 Cut, fold and fix pieces of sugarpaste to form capes.

3 Mould modelling paste face masks – comedy and tragedy.

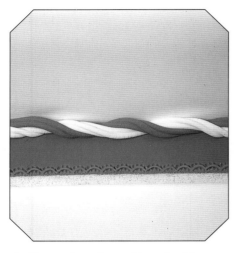

4 Cut out a modelling paste programme sheet and write text of choice with a food pen.

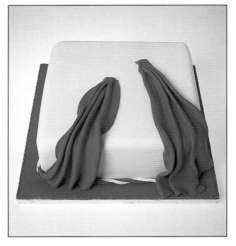

5 Fix the masks and programme to the cake-top. Then make and fix sugarpaste cape.

6 Cut and fix a second cape and then the button.

# TIME FOR TEA

Sponge cake baked in a 1.2Lt
 pudding basin (2pt)
1.25k sugarpaste (2½lb)
225g modelling paste (8oz)
Assorted food colours

28cm square cake board (11in)
 2 required
Cake card
Blossom cutter

Leaf cutter
Round cutter
Spaghetti strands
Doyley

1 Cover board with sugarpaste to form table cloth. Trim sponge to tea-pot shape, then cover with sugarpaste. Fix sugarpaste rim around top. Place onto the doyley then board.

2 Make spout and handle with modelling paste. Fix to the tea-pot when dry.

3 Make and fix 2 sugarpaste mouse heads, as shown. Use spaghetti strands for the whiskers.

4 Make the tea-pot lid with modelling paste and fix. Decorate with sugarpaste blossoms made with a blossom cutter.

5 Cut and fix further blossoms around the tea-pot together with sugarpaste leaves.

6 Make sugarpaste biscuits, with one biscuit nibbled.

# ROSIE LEA

## INGREDIENTS

Sponge cake baked in a 1.2Lt
 pudding basin (2pt)
680g sugarpaste (1½lb)
115g modelling paste (4oz)

115g royal icing (4oz)
Caramel and blue food
 colours

## EQUIPMENT and DECORATIONS

15cm round cake board (6in)
Plate or saucer
Fine paint brush
Birthday card

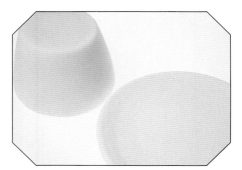

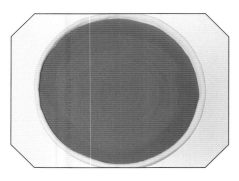

1 Upturn the sponge onto the cake board and cover with sugarpaste. Then cover a saucer or plate, of appropriate size, with sugarpaste. Leave to dry.

2 Using modelling paste, make a cup handle and spoon. Leave to dry.

3 When sugarpaste is dry, upturn cup and remove cake board. Fill-in top with softened royal icing or buttercream to form tea. Fix handle. Decorate cup and saucer with painted flowers.

# POST BOX

**1** Cover board with decorative board covering. Cut a slice off the swiss roll for the top. Stand swiss roll on end and cover with sugarpaste. Pipe design shown, with royal icing (No.2). Leave until dry.

**2** Fix a strip of sugarpaste down the side and over the piped design. Using the modelling tool, impress design as shown. Cut out and fix sugarpaste opening and base.

**3** Cover the slice with sugarpaste and fix to cake-top. Fix post box to the round card, then to board. Decorate the oblong card with sugarpaste and royal icing (No.1) to form a letter.

## INGREDIENTS

Large swiss roll
680g sugarpaste (1½lb)
115g royal icing (4oz)
Assorted food colours

## EQUIPMENT and DECORATIONS

28cm square cake board (11in)
Decorative board covering
Small round cake card
Small oblong cake card
Piping tubes No.1 and 2
Modelling tool

# BLUEBELL TIME

## INGREDIENTS

20.5cm round fruit cake (8in)
680g almond paste (1½lb)
1.25k sugarpaste (2½lb)
115g royal icing (4oz)
Assorted food colours

## EQUIPMENT and DECORATIONS

28cm round cake board (11in)     Modelling tool
Cocktail stick                   Narrow ribbon
Fine paint brush                 Ribbon bow
Piping tube No.1                 Board edge ribbon

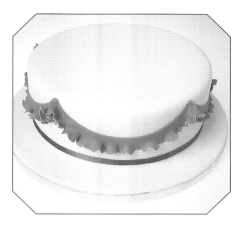

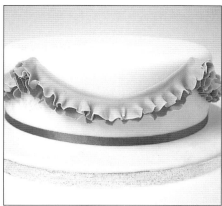

1 Cover cake and board with sugarpaste. Fix narrow ribbon around cake-base. Divide cake-side into five sections. Cut out, frill and fix, a strip of sugarpaste to each section.

2 Cut out, frill and fix, a second layer of sugarpaste over the top frill.

3 Cut out and fix a patterned strip of sugarpaste to the top. Pipe shells around the top-edge with royal icing (No.1).

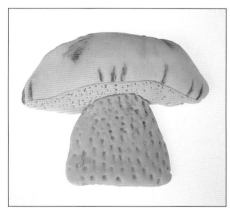

4 Using a fine paint brush, paint background scene with edible food colours, as shown.

5 Mould a large sugarpaste toadstool. Prick with the end of a paint brush to mark as shown. Paint with edible food colouring.

6 Mould body and head of the upright mouse. Fix together, then mark with a cocktail stick to form fur. Paint with food colour. Make and fix paws, ears, eyes and nose.

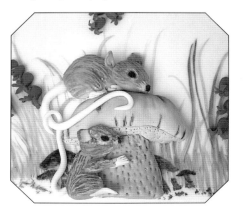

7 Repeat step 6 to form the crouching mouse.

8 Mould sugarpaste into a pear-shape. Cut and shape with fingers to form bluebells and fix to the cake-top as required.

9 Fix the toadstool and the mice to the cake-top and make and fix sugarpaste tails. Pipe inscription of choice with royal icing (No.1).

20.5cm square fruit cake (8in)
900g almond paste (2lb)
900g sugarpaste (2lb)
225g royal icing (8oz)
Blue and brown food colours

25.5cm square cake board (10in)
Fine paint brush
Piping tube No.1
Board edge ribbon

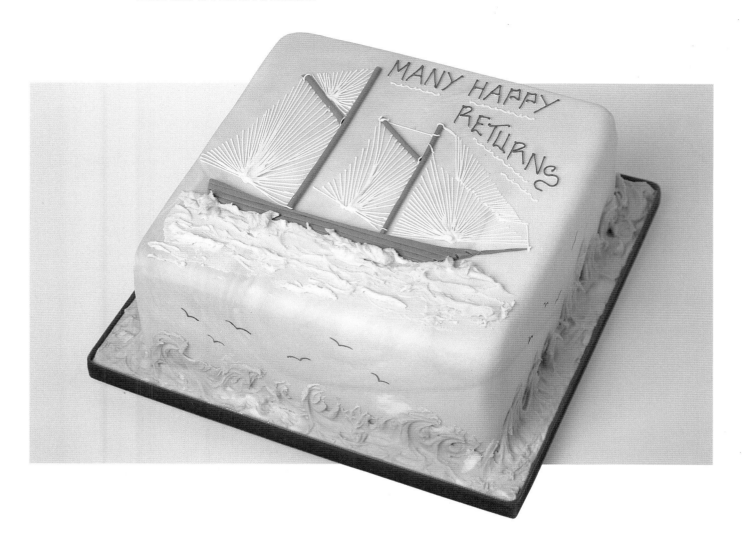

1 Cover the cake with mottled sugarpaste. Stipple royal icing around the board to form waves. Paint birds around the cake-sides.

2 Using the template as a guide, cut out and fix sugarpaste hull and masts to the cake-top. Stipple royal icing for the sea.

3 Pipe the lines as shown (No.1). Pipe inscription of choice (No.1). Fix ribbon around the cake board.

# TWINS BIRTHDAY

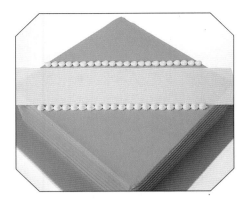

1 Coat cake and board with royal icing using a serrated scraper for sides. Leave until dry. Place a strip of paper across diagonal of cake. Pipe shells each side (No.43).

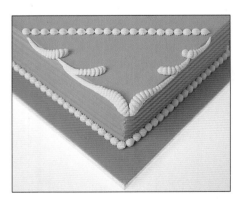

2 Pipe scrolls on opposite corners as shown. Pipe shells around the cake-base (No.43).

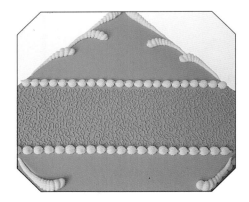

3 Pipe filigree across cake-top (No.1). Pipe decorative line around cake-board edge, then pipe inscription of choice as shown (No.1). Fix favours as required.

## INGREDIENTS

20.5cm square fruit cake (8in)
900g almond paste (2lb)
900g royal icing (2lb)
Brown and blue food colour

## EQUIPMENT and DECORATIONS

28cm square cake board (11in)
Serrated scraper
Piping tubes No.1 and 43
Favours
Board edge ribbon

# Heart's Ease

## INGREDIENTS

20.5cm round fruit cake (8in)
680g almond paste (1½lb)
900g sugarpaste (2lb)
115g royal icing (4oz)
Assorted food colours

## EQUIPMENT and DECORATIONS

28cm round cake board (11in)    Fine paint brush
Cocktail stick                  Piping tube No.1
Embosser                        Butterflies
Blossom cutters                 Board edge ribbon

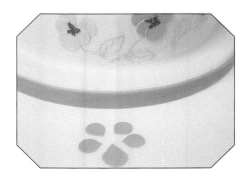

1 Cover cake and board with sugarpaste. Pipe leaves and stems around cake-side with royal icing. Cut petals from sugarpaste, as shown. Fix and decorate to make into pansies.

2 Cut, frill and fix a strip of sugarpaste to the cake-base. Roll out, emboss and fix a narrow length of sugarpaste to the cake-base.

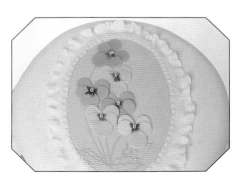

3 Make and decorate a sugarpaste plaque for the cake-top as shown. Pipe inscription of choice (No.1).

## INGREDIENTS

20.5cm round fruit cake (8in)
680g almond paste (1½lb)
1.25k sugarpaste (2½lb)
225g royal icing (8oz)
Assorted dusting powders
Assorted food colours

## EQUIPMENT and DECORATIONS

28cm round cake board (11in)
Fine paint brush
Non-stick paper
Piping tube No.1
Board edge ribbon

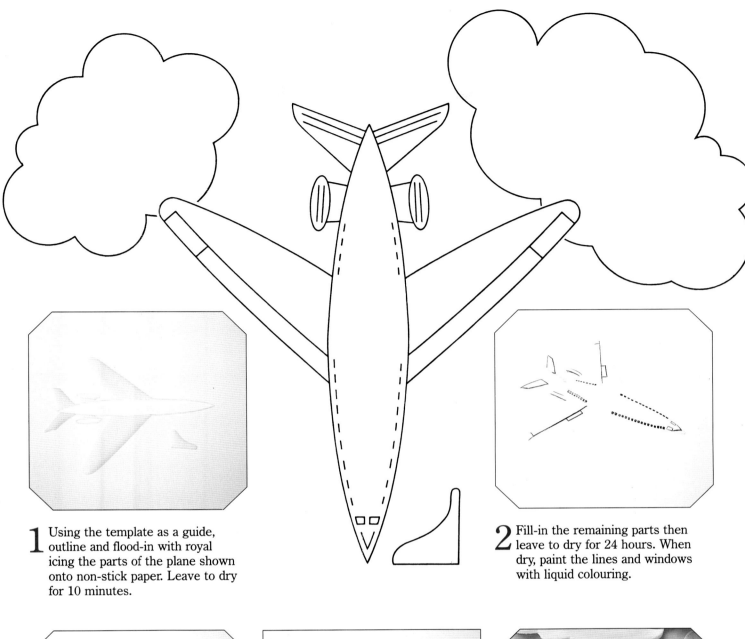

1 Using the template as a guide, outline and flood-in with royal icing the parts of the plane shown onto non-stick paper. Leave to dry for 10 minutes.

2 Fill-in the remaining parts then leave to dry for 24 hours. When dry, paint the lines and windows with liquid colouring.

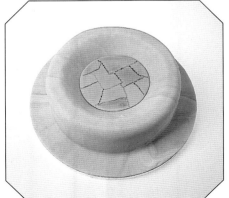

3 Cut the cake to form a hollow top, then cover with sugarpaste. Cut out and fix a sugarpaste circle in the hollow and paint in fields.

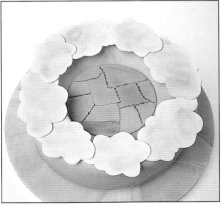

4 Cut out and fix clouds to the cake-top and colour with dusting powder.

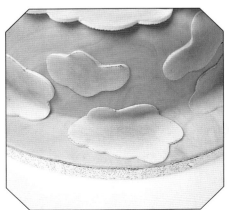

5 Cut out and fix additional clouds around cake-sides and base. When dry, fix plane across the cake-top. Pipe inscription with royal icing (No.1).

119

## INGREDIENTS

10, 15 and 20.5cm round
 fruit cakes (4, 6 and 8in)
1.5k almond paste (3lb)
2k sugarpaste (4lb)
340g modelling paste (12oz)
225g royal icing (8oz)
Assorted food colours

## EQUIPMENT and DECORATIONS

35.5cm round cake board (14in)
10cm round cake card (4in)
15cm round cake card (6in)
Piping tubes No.1 and 42
Fine paint brush
Cocktail stick

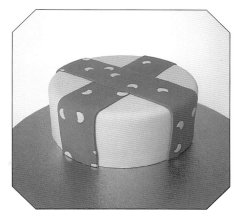

1 Cover each cake with sugarpaste, then cut out and fix sugarpaste over the cake. Decorate with crescent shaped, pieces as shown.

2 Fix the cakes together as shown. Make and fix a sugarpaste bow onto the cake-top. Pipe shells around the cake-bases with royal icing (No.42).

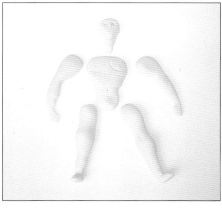

3 Mould the various parts of the body shown with sugarpaste.

4 Fix the pieces together in the seating position shown. Paint in the hair, then make and fix a sugarpaste top hat.

5 Repeat steps 3 to 4 to make as many as required.

6 Make the figure shown and fix into the centre of the bow.

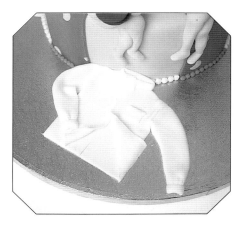

7 Make and fix a selection of sugarpaste clothing to the cake board. Pipe inscription of choice with royal icing (No.1).

# FRUIT BOWL

INGREDIENTS

Sponge cake baked in a 1.2Lt
 pudding basin (2pt)
Small sponge cakes for the fruits
900g sugarpaste (2lb)
Assorted food colours

EQUIPMENT and DECORATIONS

30.5cm round cake board (12in)
25.5cm round doyley (10in)
Leaf cutter
Fine paint brush
Clove

1 Cover the sponge side with
sugarpaste. Then cover the top of
the sponge. Make and fix two strips
of sugarpaste, twisted together,
around the top edge.

2 Cover small sponges with
sugarpaste to make a selection of
fruit, and decorate with sugarpaste
leaves and clove.

3 Fix the fruit to the top and
decorate with sugarpaste grapes.

# CAULIFLOWER LOVE

1 Layer sponges together then trim sides to curve shape. Coat with buttercream and chill in a refrigerator. When chilled cover with sugarpaste and shape with the coarse cloth.

2 Cut out sugarpaste and press with a caulifower leaf to mark the veins.

3 Cut around leaf. Thin edges with a cocktail stick then fix to sponge. Repeat steps 2 and 3 to complete cauliflower cake. Make and fix a pair of sugarpaste caterpillars as required.

INGREDIENTS

20.5cm round sponge cake (8in)
 2 required
1.5k sugarpaste (3lb)
225g royal icing (8oz)
Green, yellow and brown
 food colours

EQUIPMENT and DECORATIONS

30.5cm round cake board (12in)
Coarse cloth
Cauliflower leaves, washed
 and dried
Cocktail stick
Sugar flowers
Board edge ribbon

123

# CUPID'S STING

INGREDIENTS

23cm heart shaped fruit
 cake (9in)
1.25k almond paste (2½lb)
1.5k sugarpaste (3lb)

225g modelling paste (8oz)
115g royal icing (4oz)
Brown dusting powder
Assorted food colours

EQUIPMENT and DECORATIONS

30.5cm heart shaped cake board (12in)
Heart shaped crimper
Small heart shaped cutter
Fine paint brush
Piping tube No.1
Board edge ribbon

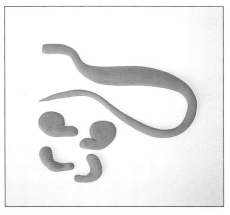

1 Cover the cake and board with sugarpaste. Then press the heart shaped crimper lightly into the paste around the cake-top edge and board, as shown.

2 Mould sugarpaste into shapes shown for a dinosaur.

3 Fix the pieces to the cake-side.

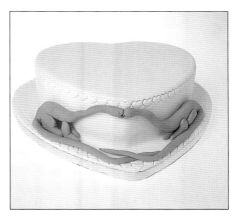

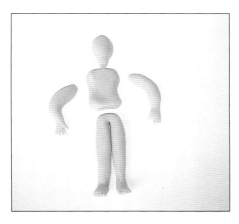

4 Repeat for opposite side, with dinosaurs meeting at the head.

5 Mould the various parts for the caveman with modelling paste.

6 Mould the various parts for the cavewoman with modelling paste.

7 Fix the caveman together. Make and decorate clothing and head. Fix to the cake-top with stippled royal icing.

8 Fix the cavewoman. Make and decorate clothing and head. Fix to the cake-top as shown.

9 Decorate cake-side with cut out sugarpaste hearts. Stipple around cake-base with royal icing. Pipe and decorate inscription of choice (No.1).

# FAIRYTALE ROMANCE

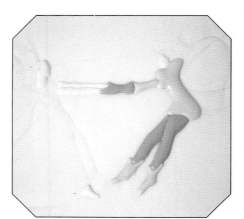

**1** Cover cake and board with sugarpaste. Leave to dry. Using template as guide, trace the picture onto cake-top. Fill in the parts shown with softened royal icing.

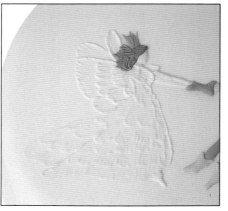

**2** Brush embroider the fairy's wings and dress (see p.25). Pipe hair and crown (No.1).

**3** Brush embroider the elf's wing, then pipe in the hair and crown (No.1).

25.5cm round fruit cake (10in)
1.25g almond paste (2½lb)
1.75k sugarpaste (3½lb)
225g royal icing (8oz)
Assorted food colours

30.5 cm round cake board (12in)   Leaf cutter
Fine paint brush                       Narrow ribbon
Piping tubes No.1 and 2          Hearts
Cocktail stick                        Motto
Blossom cutter                   Board edge ribbon

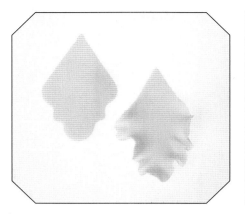

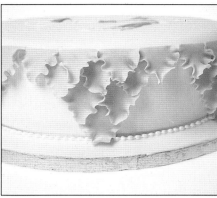

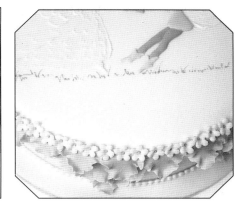

4 Fix narrow ribbon, then pipe shells around cake-base (No.2). Using template as a guide cut out sugarpaste petal shape and frill the edges with a cocktail stick.

5 Divide cake into six. Fix petal to the cake-base. Repeat step 4 to make as many petals as required to form the pattern shown. (Fix each petal when made).

6 Using blossom cutter, cut out and fix sugarpaste blossoms around cake-top edge. Then pipe a dot in each centre (No.1). Using a fine paint brush, paint grass on cake-top. Fix decorations of choice.

# ORANGE BLOSSOM

## INGREDIENTS

20.5cm round fruit cake (8in)
680g almond paste (1½lb)
680g royal icing (1½lb)
Cream, apricot and green
  food colours

## EQUIPMENT and DECORATIONS

28cm round cake board (11in)
Serrated scraper
Piping tubes No.1, 2 and 7
Decorative flowers
Board edge ribbon

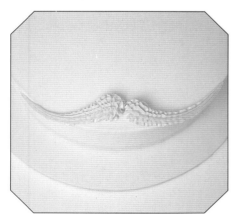

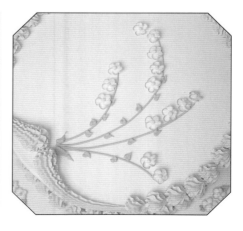

1 Coat cake, using a serrated scraper for side, and then board with royal icing. When dry, pipe two scrolls with royal icing (No.7) onto cake-top edge as shown.

2 Pipe shells around the remaining cake-top edge and then around the cake-base (No.7).

3 Pipe stems and leaves onto cake-top (No.2). Fix flowers as required. Pipe leaves on the board (No.2) and fix flowers. Pipe inscription of choice (No.1).

# VALENTINE ROSE

INGREDIENTS

25.5cm square sponge cake (10in)
1.5k sugarpaste (3lb)
115g modelling paste (4oz)
Red, green and yellow food colours

EQUIPMENT and DECORATIONS

35.5 x 25.5cm oblong cake
 board (14 x 10in)
Cake card
Decorative board covering
Flower and leaf cutters

Heart shaped cutter
Piping tube No.42
Floral wire and tape
Wide ribbon
Motto

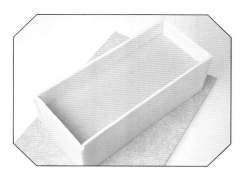  

1 Cover board with decorative paper. Cut sponge in half and layer. Fix to cake card. Cover top with sugarpaste. Cut pieces of sugarpaste and fix to cake side when dry. Fix to board.

2 Cut out and fix a thin sheet of sugarpaste into box, to give ruffled material effect. Cut out and fix sugarpaste hearts. Pipe shells with royal icing (No.42) around edges of the box.

3 Make a large rose from modelling paste and fix to taped wire. Place into the box then fix ribbon and motto as shown.

20.5cm square fruit cake (8in)
900g almond paste (2lb)
680g royal icing (1½lb)
680g sugarpaste (1½lb)
Assorted food colours

25.5cm square cake board (10in)
Piping tube No.1
Flowers and leaves
Board edge ribbon

1 Coat the cake with royal icing. When dry, cover the cake-top with sugarpaste squares.

2 Cut out and fix a strip of sugarpaste to the cake-base and then the board.

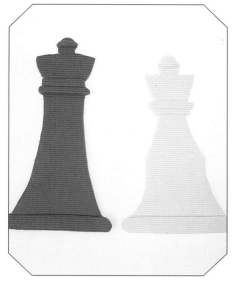

3 Using the templates as a guide, cut out a sugarpaste King and Queen.

4 Fix the figures to the cake-top and decorate as shown.

5 Trace the small chess figures onto paper, cut out and place onto the squares. Pipe a line around the paper figures (No.1) leave to dry then remove the paper.

6 Make sugarpaste plaques and pipe message of choice (No.1). Decorate the cake corners with flowers and leaves.

# FANTASIA

## INGREDIENTS

20.5cm round fruit cake (8in)
680g almond paste (1½lb)
900g sugarpaste (2lb)
French pink and green food
 colours

## EQUIPMENT and DECORATIONS

28cm round cake board (11in)   Cocktail stick
Crimper                        Ribbon bow
Fine paint brush               Motto
Flower cutter                  Board edge ribbon
Butterfly cutter

1 Cover cake and board with sugarpaste. Immediately crimp around
board edge, to make the pattern
shown. When dry, paint stems and
leaves from board to the cake-top.

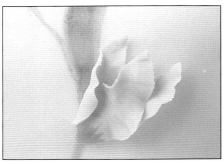

2 Cut out, frill with a cocktail stick
and fix sugarpaste flowers to the
stem.

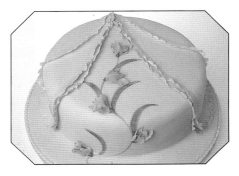

3 Cut out, frill and fix strips of
sugarpaste over the cake, as
shown. Make and fix sugarpaste
butterflies. Fix ribbon bow
and motto.

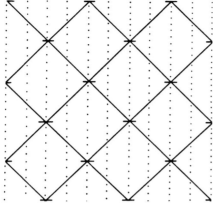

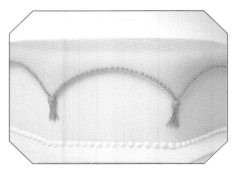

1 Cover cake and board with sugar-paste. When dry, cover cake-top and sides with a second layer of sugarpaste and trim to shape shown. Fix in position. Pipe shells around cake-base (No.2).

2 Pipe shells along the edge of the sugarpaste as shown (No.1). Pipe a tassel onto the bottom of each curve.

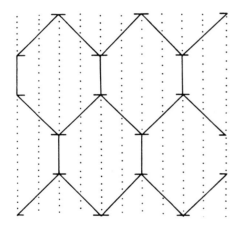

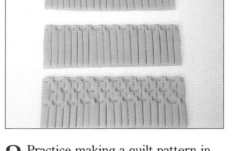

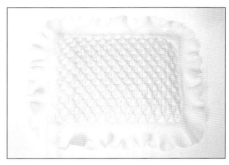

3 Practice making a quilt pattern in the following sequence: roll out sugarpaste and mark narrow lines with back of a knife. Squeeze paste with tweezers on alternate lines. Alternate marks for each line.

4 Make a quilted sugarpaste pillow using the sequence in step 3. Cut out, frill and fix a strip of sugarpaste around the pillow edge.

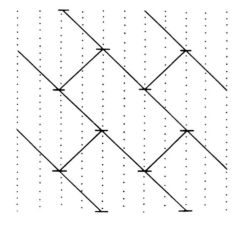

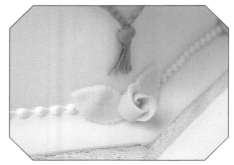

5 Pipe lines with royal icing (No.1) to form the criss-cross design then pipe a short, horizontal line over each join. Pipe shells around the edge as shown.

6 Make and fix a sugarpaste rose spray to each cake-base corner. Decorate the cake with appropriate favours.

20.5cm hexagonal fruit cake (8in)
900g almond paste (2lb)
1.5k sugarpaste (3lb)
225g royal icing (8oz)
Pink food colour

28cm hexagonal shaped cake
  board (11in)
Piping tubes No.1 and 2
Tweezers

Cocktail stick
Leaf cutter
Favours
Board edge ribbon

## INGREDIENTS

20.5cm square fruit cake (8in)
900g almond paste (2lb)
680g sugarpaste (1½lb)
225g modelling paste (8oz)
115g royal icing (4oz)
French pink food colour

## EQUIPMENT and DECORATIONS

28cm square cake board (11in)
Piping tubes No.1 and 2
Frill cutters
Cocktail stick
Miniature heart shaped cutter
Floral sprays
Ribbon bows
Miniature horseshoes
Board edge ribbon

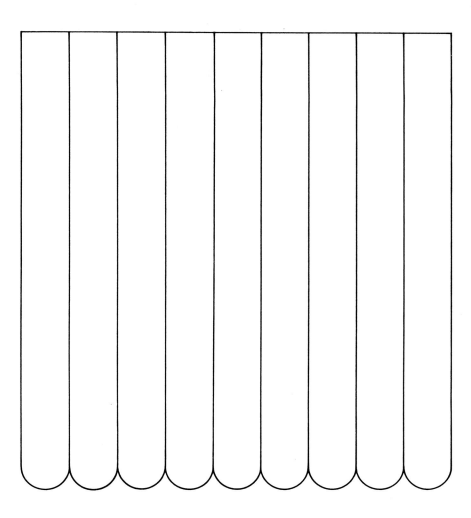

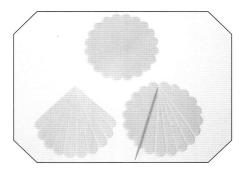

1 Cover cake and board with sugarpaste. Pipe shells around cake-base (No.2). Cut out a fluted circle of sugarpaste. Mark with a cocktail stick then cut into fan shape shown.

2 Fix to the cake corner to form a corner vase. Make and fix a vase for each corner. Then make and fix small fan shapes to each cake-side.

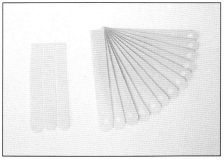

3 Using the template as a guide, cut lengths of modelling paste, cut out a miniature heart from each length and then fix together to make a fan.

4 Fix fan to cake-top and pipe tassels with royal icing (No.1) then pipe a decorative line around board edge. Fill vases with floral sprays. Pipe inscription of choice (No.1).

# PASSIONATE HARES

### INGREDIENTS

20.5cm long octagonal fruit cake (8in)
900g almond paste (2lb)
1.5k sugarpaste (3lb)
115g royal icing (4oz)
Assorted food colours

### EQUIPMENT and DECORATIONS

25.5cm long octagonal
  shaped cake board (10in)
Endless cutter
Piping tube No.1

Crimper
Birthday ribbon
Sugar flowers
Board edge ribbon

1 Cover the cake and board with sugarpaste. Cut out and fix a sugarpaste top. Fix ribbon around the cake board edge.

2 Cut out and fix a sugarpaste band around the cake-side. Make and fix a sugarpaste disc to the cake-top. Fix ribbons as shown.

3 Make and fix a pair of sugarpaste hares. Pipe inscription of choice with royal icing (No.1). Decorate with sugar flowers.

30.5cm petal shaped fruit cake (12in)
2k almond paste (4lb)
2.5k sugarpaste (5lb)
450g royal icing (1lb)
Pink and green food colours

35.5cm petal shaped cake board (14in)
Piping tubes No.1, 2 and 42
Heart shaped cutter
Floral spray
Board edge ribbon

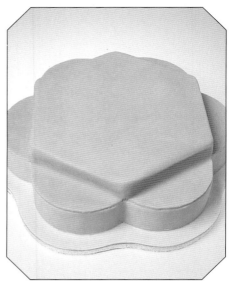

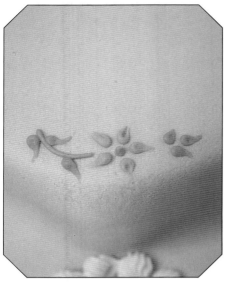

1 Cut, then cover the cake with sugarpaste as shown. Place onto the board and then coat the board with royal icing. Leave to dry for 4 hours.

2 Pipe a floral design around the cake-side (No.1) then pipe shells around the cake-top and base (No.42).

3 Pipe the floral design onto the cake-top corners (No.1).

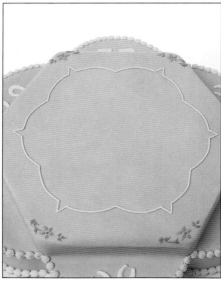

4 Cut out sugarpaste heart and horseshoe shapes and fix to the cake.

5 Pipe the line shown on the cake-top (No.2).

6 Pipe lines and leaves beside the cake-top line (No.1). Make and fix a posey of artificial flowers as required.

Increase or decrease the
template to suit the size of
the cake being decorated.

## INGREDIENTS

23cm petal shaped fruit cake (9in)
900g almond paste (2lb)
1.5k sugarpaste (3lb)
115g royal icing (4oz)
Assorted food colours

## EQUIPMENT and DECORATIONS

30.5cm petal shaped cake board (12in)     Cocktail stick
Fluted cutter                             Piping tube No.1
Tulle                                     Ribbon bow
Blossom cutter                            Board edge ribbon

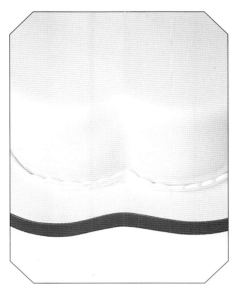

1 Cover the cake and board with sugarpaste. Cut out and fix a fluted strip of sugarpaste around the cake-base.

2 Cut and fix lengths of sugarpaste around the cake-side. Cut out and fix small fluted sugarpaste circles as shown.

3 Cut out a larger fluted circle of sugarpaste then frill the edge with a cocktail stick.

4 Frill another circle of sugarpaste and fix into first circle. Roll out a ball of sugarpaste and mark with tulle to form flower centre. Make as many flowers as required.

5 Cut out a square of sugarpaste and ruche into a triangular shape.

6 Place onto cake-top and fill with flowers. Cut and fix lengths of sugarpaste for the stems and leaves. Fix a ribbon bow. Pipe inscription of choice (No.1).

**1** Using the scallop shell as a mould, make 2 shells with modelling paste. Leave until dry.

**2** When the shells are hard and dry fix gypsophila, flowers and ribbon loops into the bottom shell, as shown.

**3** Brush the top shell with dusting powder and fix onto the filled shell.

20.5cm square fruit cake (8in)
900g almond paste (2lb)
1.25k sugarpaste (2½lb)
225 modelling paste (8oz)
225g royal icing (8oz)
Dusting powder
Cream and apricot food colours

28cm square cake board (11in)
Piping tubes No.1, 2 and 3
Crimper
Non-stick paper
Dried gypsophila
Assorted flowers
Ribbon loops
Scallop shell
Motto
Board edge ribbon

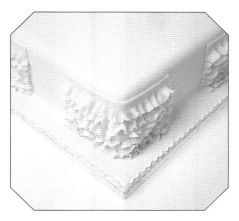

**4** Cover cake and board with sugarpaste. Crimp around board edge. Cut, and frill with a cocktail stick, strips of sugarpaste then fix to corners in layers as shown.

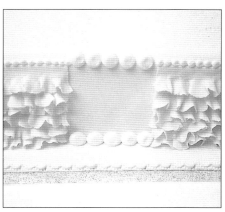

**5** Pipe bulbs between the frills along the cake-top edge and base (No.3). Pipe shells on the top edge of the frills (No.2).

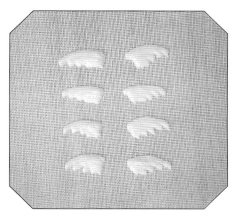

**6** Pipe 4 left and 4 right wings (No.1) onto non-stick paper and leave until dry.

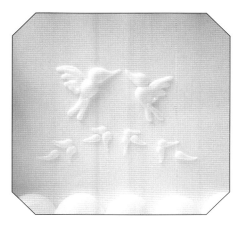

**7** When the wings are dry, pipe floral design and 2 birds on one side of the cake (No.1).

**8** Immediately fix a wing into each bird. Repeat step 7 and 8 for each side. Pipe a line over the bulbs (No.2) then overpipe the No.2 line (No.1).

**9** Fix the filled shell to the cake-top. Decorate the cake-top as required.

# 50TH ANNIVERSARY

## INGREDIENTS

18 x 30.5cm oblong fruit
 cake (7 x 12in)
20.5cm oval fruit cake (8in)
2k almond paste (4lb)
2.25k sugarpaste (4½lb)
Yellow food colour

## EQUIPMENT and DECORATIONS

25.5 x 35.5cm cake board (10 x 14in)
20.5cm oval cake card (8in)
Crimper
Daisy cutter
Tulle or sieve

Yellow food pen
Narrow ribbon
Ribbon bows
Motto
Board edge ribbon

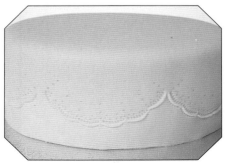

1 Cover one cake with sugarpaste, mark the side with a crimper, then make the dots using the food pen. Repeat the same process for the remaining cake.

2 Cut out sugarpaste daisy shapes, cut down middle of each petal then press with a cocktail stick. Make and fix a sugarpaste centre. Make as many flowers as required.

3 Fix the cakes together onto the cake board and then cover the board with sugarpaste. Crimp the edge. Fix ribbons, bows, flowers and favours.

# DIAMOND WEDDING

**1** Cover the cake and board with sugarpaste. Cut fluted circles of sugarpaste, frill the edge then fold in half and fix around the cake-base.

**2** Pipe decorative floral pattern around the cake-top edge with royal icing (No.1).

**3** Cut out and fix small sugarpaste blossoms to form numerals shown. Pipe a dot in each centre (No.1). Decorate corner with blossoms and piped leaves (No.1).

## INGREDIENTS

25.5 x 15cm diamond shaped
 fruit cake (10 x 6in)
900g almond paste (2lb)
900g sugarpaste (2lb)
115g royal icing (4oz)
Blue food colour

## EQUIPMENT and DECORATIONS

30.5 x 20.5cm diamond shaped
 cake board (12 x 8in)
Fluted cutter
Cocktail stick
Piping tube No.1
Blossom cutter
Board edge ribbon

# PLATINUM ANNIVERSARY

INGREDIENTS

20.5cm round fruit cake (8in)
900g almond paste (2lb)
1.5k sugarpaste (3lb)
115g modelling paste (4oz)
Blue food colour

EQUIPMENT and DECORATIONS

33cm round cake board (13in)
Modelling tool
Cocktail stick
Small blossom cutter

Floral wire and tape
Narrow ribbons
Dried gypsophila
Board edge ribbon

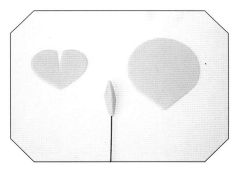

1 Using template as a guide, cut cake in half in the shape shown. Cover with sugarpaste. Using template as a guide, cut out and fix sugarpaste band around the cake-base.

2 Cut out and fix a sugarpaste band around the cake-top edge.

3 Using templates as guide, cut out a heart and petal shape from modelling paste. Then fix modelling paste to wire in the shape shown. Cut the heart as shown.

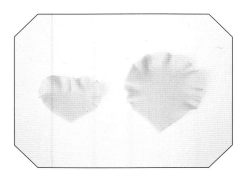

4 Frill the top edge of the heart and petal, using a cocktail stick.

5 Fix the pieces together to form a sweetpea.

6 Make varying sizes of sweetpeas and tape together. Make and fix tape tendrils.

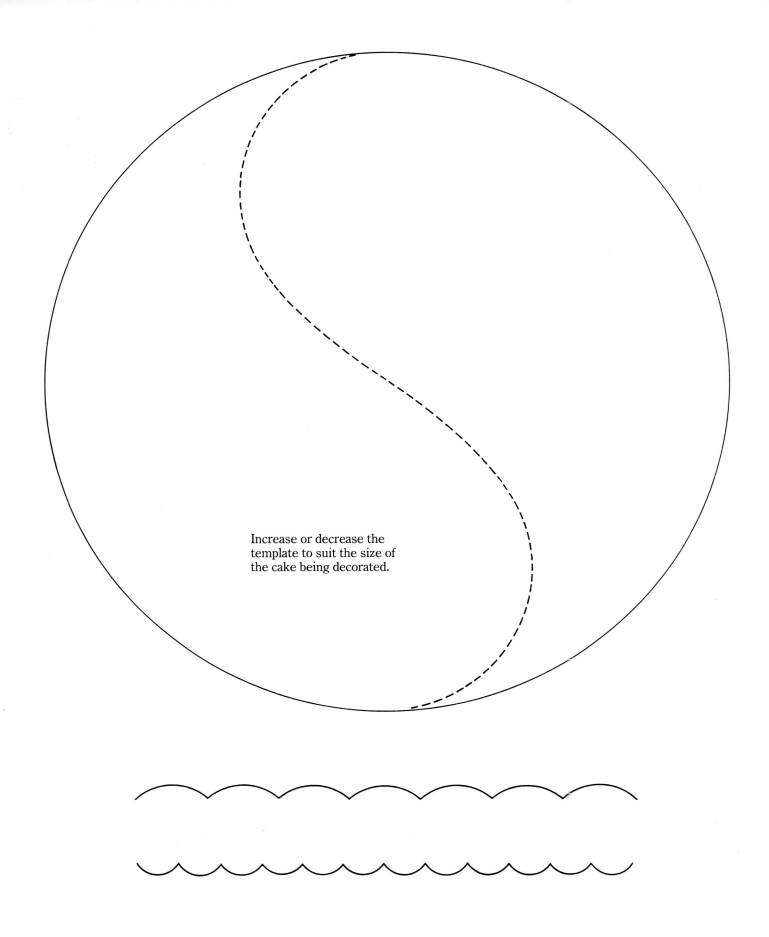

Increase or decrease the
template to suit the size of
the cake being decorated.

# FLORAL FILIGREE

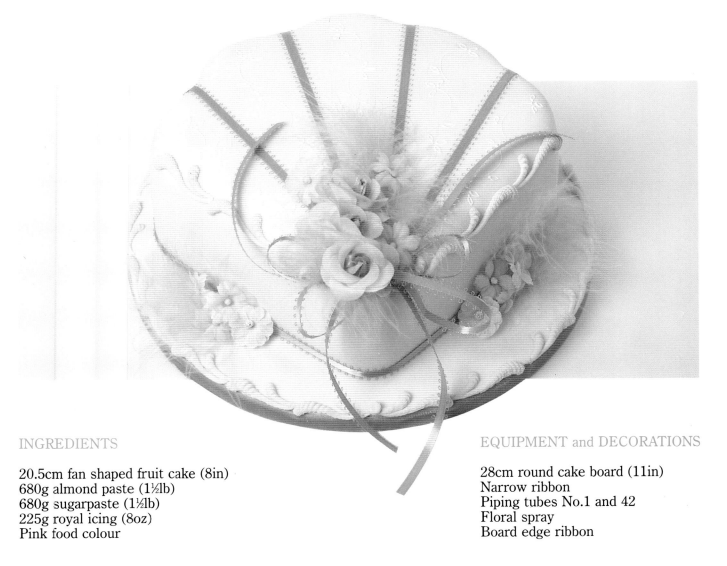

INGREDIENTS

20.5cm fan shaped fruit cake (8in)
680g almond paste (1½lb)
680g sugarpaste (1½lb)
225g royal icing (8oz)
Pink food colour

EQUIPMENT and DECORATIONS

28cm round cake board (11in)
Narrow ribbon
Piping tubes No.1 and 42
Floral spray
Board edge ribbon

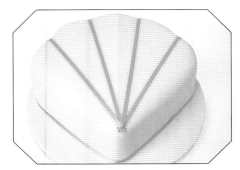

1 Cover the cake and board with sugarpaste. Fix narrow ribbon as shown.

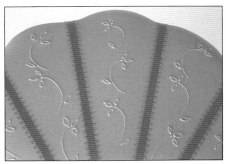

2 Pipe a floral design between the ribbons on the cake-top with royal icing (No.1).

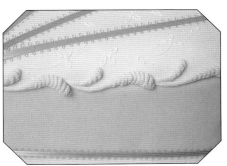

3 Pipe scrolls around the cake-top edge and board (No.42). Fix floral sprays as required.

## INGREDIENTS

20.5cm round fruit cake (8in)
680g almond paste (1½lb)
680g sugarpaste (1½lb)
115g modelling paste (4oz)
115g royal icing (4oz)
Assorted food colours

## EQUIPMENT and DECORATIONS

28cm round cake board (11in)
Crimper
Piping tubes No.1, 2 and 3
Fine paint brush
Non-stick paper
Sugar flowers
Board edge ribbon

  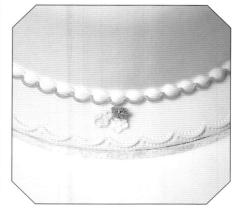

**1** Using the templates as a guide, cut out the two crows from modelling paste. When dry, brush with food colours using a fine paint brush.

**2** Cover the cake and board with sugarpaste. Crimp around the board edge. Paint in the ground, fix the crows, then make and fix a pie.

**3** Pipe bulbs around cake-base (No.3). Pipe a line against bulbs (No.2). Decorate board with sugar flowers. Pipe inscription of choice on cake-top (No.1).

# GRANDMA

INGREDIENTS

20.5cm round fruit cake (8in)
680g almond paste (1½lb)
900g royal icing (2lb)
Assorted food colours

EQUIPMENT and DECORATIONS

28cm round cake board (11in)     Leaf piping tube
Food approved pens               Non-stick paper
Piping tubes No.1, 2, 3 and 57   Cocktail stick
Fine paint brush                 Board edge ribbon

1 Coat the cake and board with royal icing. When dry, draw floral design around the cake-side and board, using the food approved pens.

2 **For the daffodil**: Pipe the petals shown (No.57) onto non-stick paper, using royal icing.

3 Using a cocktail stick, draw along centre of each petal to create shape shown. Pipe a spiral line (No.2) to form centre. 7 daffodils required. Leave until dry.

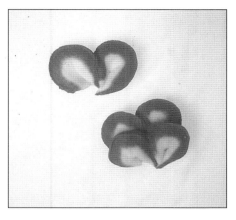

4 **For the pansy**: Fill a piping bag with two colours of royal icing and pipe the petals (No.57) onto non-stick paper.

5 Pipe a large petal below the four smaller petals. 5 pansies required. When dry, colour the centre as shown.

6 Pipe leaves, using a cut piping bag or leaf shaped tube, onto the cake-top and fix the flowers.

7 Pipe shells around the cake-top edge and base (No.3).

8 Pipe a line over the shells (No.2) then overpipe the No.2 line (No.1).

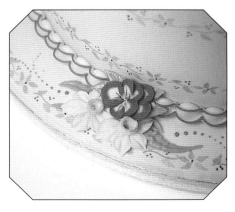

9 Pipe a few leaves onto the board and fix flowers to form a spray. Pipe inscription of choice (No.1).

# GRANDAD

INGREDIENTS

25.5cm oval fruit cake (10in)
1.25k almond paste (2½lb)
1.25k sugarpaste (2½lb)
115g royal icing (4oz)
Brown and green food colours

EQUIPMENT and DECORATIONS

30.5cm oval cake board (12in)
Fine paint brush
Pointed knife
Piping tube No.1

Narrow ribbon
Miniature horseshoes
Board edge ribbon

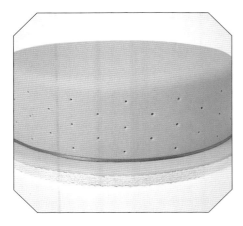

1 Cover cake and board with sugarpaste. Using template as a guide, punch small holes around cake-side in an even pattern. Leave until dry. Fix narrow ribbon around cake-base.

2 Using the template as a guide trace the outline onto the cake-top and brush-in with colouring, as shown. Leave to dry.

3 Pipe floral pattern around the cake-side with royal icing (No.1). Scratch painting of the horse with pointed knife to create effect shown. Pipe inscription of choice with royal icing (No.1).

# GARDENER'S BARROW

20.5cm round fruit cake (8in)
680g almond paste (1½lb)
900g sugarpaste (2lb)
115g royal icing (4oz)
Assorted dusting powders
Assorted food colours

28cm round cake board (11in)
Fine sponge
Fine paint brush
Piping tubes No.1 and 3
Board edge ribbon

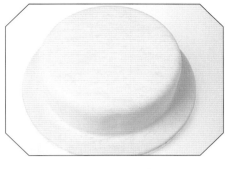

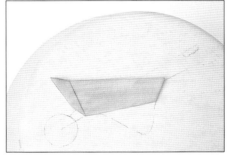

1 Cover the cake with sugarpaste and stipple with liquid colouring, using a fine sponge.

2 Using the template as a guide, cut out sugarpaste border, fix to the cake-base and colour with dusting powders.

3 Trace the template onto the cake-top. Cut out and fix the wheelbarrow body from sugarpaste.

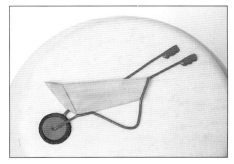

4 Make and fix the wheel then pipe the lines (No.3).

5 Make and fix various sugarpaste vegetable shapes.

6 Make and fix various sugarpaste vegetables around the cake board.

7 Pipe inscription of choice (No.1). Fix ribbon around the board.

# WEDDING PORTRAIT

## INGREDIENTS

15 and 20.5cm oval fruit
 cakes (6 and 8in)
1.5k almond paste (3lb)
2k sugarpaste (4lb)
115g royal icing (4oz)
225g modelling paste (8oz)
Assorted dusting powders
Assorted food colours

## EQUIPMENT and DECORATIONS

23 and 30.5cm oval cake
 boards (9 and 12in)
Crimper
Narrow ribbon
Cocktail stick
String pearls
Fine paint brush
Decorations of choice
Board edge ribbon

1 Cover cakes with sugarpaste, then around board edge with a second colour and crimp. When dry, fix narrow ribbon around cake-base.

2 Make and fix three layers of frilled sugarpaste, starting low and rising to join together in a folded pattern.

3 Fix string pearls and loops with royal icing as shown.

4 Using the template as a guide, transfer the design onto a modelling paste plaque. Outline in two colours.

5 Brush-in figures with dusting powders. Fix plaque to a larger modelling paste plaque, frilled around edge. When dry, lean plaque on a wedge of paste to display.

# FLORAL MARRIAGE

### INGREDIENTS

15cm round fruit cake (6in)
25.5cm square fruit cake (10in)
2.25k almond paste (4½lb)
2.25k royal icing (4½lb)
Salmon pink and cream food
 colours

### EQUIPMENT and DECORATIONS

15cm round cake card (6in)
33cm square cake board (13in)
Piping tubes No.1, 2, 3 and 43
Floral spray top ornament
Assorted favours
Board edge ribbon

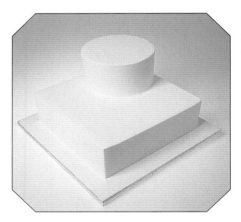

**1** Coat cakes separately with royal icing. When dry, fix cake card to round cake then fix to one corner of square cake. Then coat board with royal icing. Leave until dry.

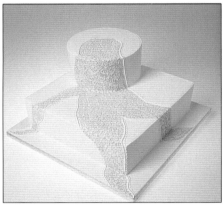

**2** Pipe irregular lines from cake-top to the board (No.2) then pipe filigree as shown (No.1). Pipe a scalloped line beside the No.2 line (No.1).

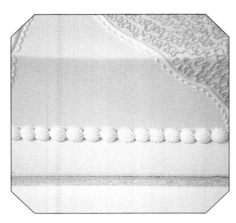

**3** Pipe shells around each cake-base (No.43).

**4** Pipe scrolls around each cake-top edge (No.43).

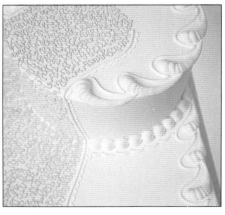

**5** Pipe a rope line beside the shells (No.2) and a line beside the scrolls (No.2).

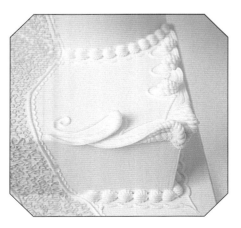

**6** Over-pipe the scrolls (No.2). Fix favours and floral spray, as required.

# ROSE GARLAND

INGREDIENTS

30.5cm petal shaped fruit cake (12in)
2k almond paste (4lb)
2.25k sugarpaste (4½lb)
225g royal icing (8oz)
Peach food colour

EQUIPMENT and DECCRATIONS

35.5cm round cake board (14in)
Piping tube No.43
Small rose leaf cutter
Floral wire and tape
Bride and Groom

164

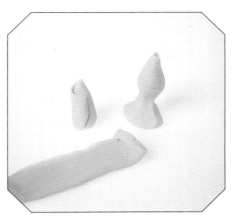

1 Cover cakes with sugarpaste. When dry, scratch a guide line onto each side then pipe shells around cake-base with royal icing (No.43).

2 Cut and twist lengths of sugarpaste, then fix onto the guidelines and down the joins. Fix strips of twisted sugarpaste to the cake-top.

3 Roll out sugarpaste as shown, roll up into a bud and pinch in the base to form a rose bud.

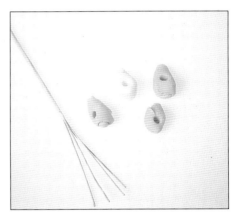

4 Make and fix as many rose buds, leaves and bows around the cake-sides as required.

5 Make and fix as many rose buds and leaves as required for the cake-top.

6 Tape 4 lengths of wire together leaving each end un-taped to form the base of arch. Make small rose buds, make a hole through sides then cut off the bases.

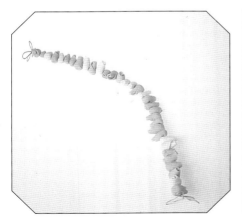

7 Thread the buds onto the wire then splay out the wire at each end.

8 Fix the arch to the cake-top with rose buds.

9 Cut and fix sugarpaste rose leaves. Then fix the bride and groom into position.

# CHURCH BELLS

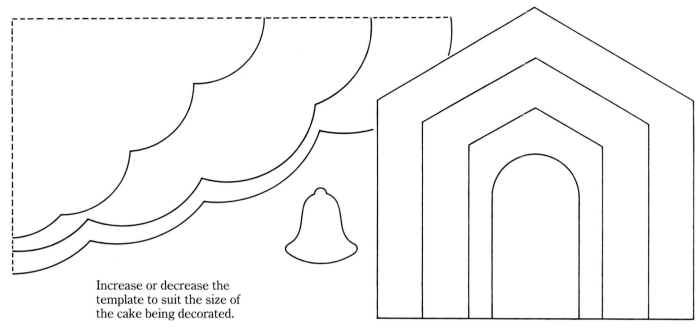

Increase or decrease the
template to suit the size of
the cake being decorated.

1 Cover the cakes with white
sugarpaste. Place on the boards,
then cover the remaining part of
the boards with blue sugarpaste.

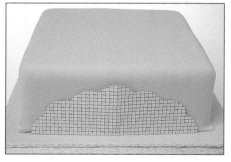

2 Cut out templates to fit cake-sides.
Cover cakes with blue sugarpaste
fixing top and corners only, then
mark around templates as shown.

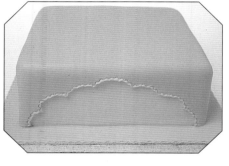

3 Cut along the mark and remove the
piece of sugarpaste. Immediately
crimp the edge.

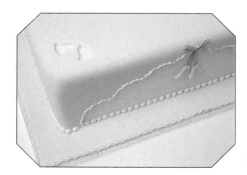

4 Cut out bell shapes from the
corners. Fix ribbons and bells to
each cake-side. Pipe shells along
cake-bases with royal icing (No.2).

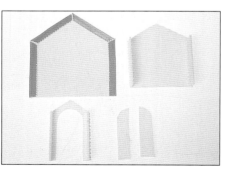

5 Using the template as a guide, cut
out the pieces shown from
modelling paste. Decorate with
ribbon and piped shells (No.1).

6 When dry, assemble pieces as
shown. Fix to a modelling paste
base and then pipe shells around
edge (No.2). Decorate with ribbon
and lace.

15, 20.5 and 25.5cm square
 fruit cakes (6, 8 and 10in)
3.5k almond paste (7lb)
5k sugarpaste (10lb)
225g royal icing (8oz)
115g modelling paste (4oz)
Blue food colour

23, 28 and 33cm square cake
 boards (9, 11 and 13in)
Bell shaped cutters
Piping tubes No.1 and 2
Crimper
Narrow ribbons
Ribbon bows
Lace
Artificial flowers
Board edge ribbon

13, 18 and 25.5cm square
 fruit cakes (5, 7 and 10in)
3k almond paste (6lb)
3k sugarpaste (6lb)
900g royal icing (2lb)
Orange food colour

20.5 and 25.5cm round cake
 boards (8 and 10in) for the
 top tier
25.5 and 30.5cm round cake
 boards (10 and 12in) for
 the middle tier
40.5 and 35.5cm round cake
 boards (16 and 14in) for
 bottom tier

Piping tubes No.1 and 2
Artificial flower
Dried Gypsophila
Ribbon bows
Horseshoes
Board edge ribbon

**1** Fix the boards together and then cover the cakes with sugarpaste.

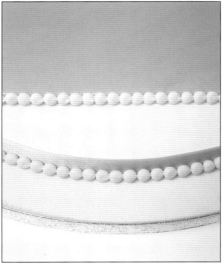

**2** Coat boards with royal icing and leave until dry. Fix ribbon around small boards then pipe shells around the cake-base and ribbon edge (No.2).

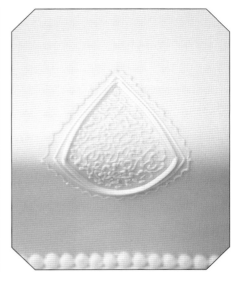

**3** Pipe the lines and filigree, as shown, on each centre of the cake-top edge (No.2 and 1).

**4** Pipe the curved lines shown on each cake-top corner (No.2).

**5** Pipe leaves and flower heads (No.1).

**6** Pipe floral designs around the cake boards (No.1). Decorate the cake with artificial flowers and horseshoes.

# CRYSTALLISED FLOWERS

Crystallised flowers are ideal for cake decorations. Elegant and very beautiful, they are suprisingly easy to make and really add that extra special feature to a cake design.

Before starting, check that the flowers you intend to crystallise are edible and have not been sprayed with pesticide.

There are many edible flowers and leaves to choose from and you will probably find a selection in the garden (see list below). Flowers from any bulb such as daffodils, snowdrops or lily-of-the-valley should never be used.

Carefully select the flowers you intend to crystallise and pick when they have just opened and are completely dry (usually around midday). Make sure that they are free from insects and discard any that are not perfect.

The flowers crystallised by the method shown here should be used within a few days. However, if you want flowers to last much longer, they may be prepared by dissolving one teaspoon of gum arabic in 25ml (1fl. oz) of water or clear alcohol such as vodka. Then paint each petal with the mixture and proceed as from step 2 shown on this page. Flowers crystallised in this manner will keep for several months.

Crystallised flowers make very attractive winter decorations when fresh flowers are hard to find for cakes and may also be used for place or table settings.

Crystallised flowers are very fragile and should be handled with extreme care. For that reason, it is wise to crystallise extra flowers in case of breakage.

1 Mix 2 teaspoons cold water with 1 fresh egg white. Gently brush the flower petals with solution using soft, medium paint brush.

2 Sprinkle with caster sugar and shake off excess. Coat the back of the petals with the egg white and water solution.

3 Sprinkle with caster sugar. Place flowers on wire tray for 24 hours to dry.

## CRYSTALLISING THROUGH THE SEASONS

SPRING
Almond blossom
Apple blossom
Chamomile
Cherry blossom
Daisy
Heartsease
Honeysuckle
Japonica
Lemon Balm
Majoram
Mint
Pansy

Parsley
Pear blossom
Polyanthus
Primula
Primrose
Sage
Violet

SUMMER
Borage
Carnation
Chive
Cornflower

Evening Primrose
Hibiscus
Honeysuckle
Hyssop
Jasmine
Lavender
Lime Marigold
Mimosa
Nasturtium
Passionflower
Pink
Rose
Rosemary

Scented Leaf
  Pelagonium

AUTUMN
Clove pink
Nasturtium
Pansy
Single
  Chrysanthemum

WINTER
Jasmine
Freesia

# ELEGANCE

15 and 25.5cm hexagonal
 shaped fruit cakes (6 and 10in)
2.5k almond paste (5lb)
2.5k sugarpaste (5lb)
225g royal icing (8oz)
Pink and ivory food colours

23 and 35.5cm hexagonal
 shaped cake boards (9 and 14in)
Crimper
Piping tubes No.1 and 2
Leaf cutters
Crystallised flowers
Ribbon loops
Board edge ribbon

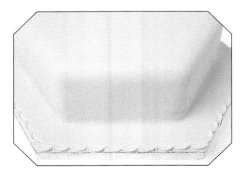

1 Cover the cake and board with sugarpaste, then immediately crimp around the edge. Repeat for second cake. Leave until dry.

2 Pipe curved lines of shells around cake-side with royal icing (No.2). Pipe a line over the shells (No.1). Pipe bows as shown (No.1).

3 Decorate the cakes with ribbon loops, sugarpaste leaves and crystallised fresh flowers fixed with royal icing.

25.5cm petal shaped fruit cake (10in)
1.5k almond paste (3lb)
2.5k sugarpaste (5lb)
115g royal icing (4oz)
Pink and silver food colours

30.5cm petal shaped cake board (12in)
Piping tube No.1
Blossom cutter
Sugar doves and bells
Board edge ribbon

**1** Roll out and cut a strip of sugarpaste then fold it in half, as shown.

**2** Fix the folded sugarpaste to the side of the cake, using a brush moistened with cooled, boiled water. Trim the ends to fit.

**3** Repeat steps 1 and 2 to cover the sides with layers to form pleats.

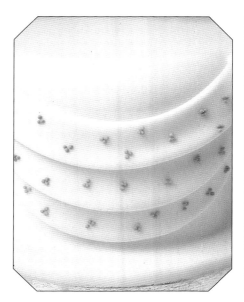

**4** When dry, pipe 3 dots in groups over the pleats with royal icing (No.1).

**5** Make and fix sugarpaste scrolls, then pipe monogram (No.1). Colour as required.

**6** Cut out and fix sugarpaste flowers and then pipe dots and scrolls (No.1). Pipe inscription of choice (No.1) and the decorate top as required.

# SPECIAL DAY

## INGREDIENTS

18 and 25.5cm square fruit
  cakes (7 and 10in)
2.5k almond paste (5lb)
2.5k sugarpaste (5lb)
115g royal icing (4oz)
Pink and green food colours

## EQUIPMENT and DECORATIONS

23 and 33cm square cake
  boards (9 and 13in)
Round cutters
Blossom cutters
Cocktail stick
Piping tubes No.1, 2 and 3
Board edge ribbon

1 Cover the cake with sugarpaste. Cut out and frill one large and one small disc of sugarpaste.

2 Fix discs together then fold and fix to the cake-base. Repeat to fill the cake-bases.

3 Make a paper template, then pipe around the edge as shown (No.3).

4 Remove the template. Pipe a line beside the No.3 line (No.1) then pipe the pattern shown (No.1).

5 Make and fix sugarpaste flowers to the cake-top edge and decorate (No.1).

6 Cut out, frill with a cocktail stick and fix sugarpaste discs to cake-top centre and decorate as shown to form flower (No.1).

20.5 and 28cm petal shaped
 fruit cakes (8 and 11in)
2.5k almond paste (5lb)
4k sugarpaste (8lb)
115g royal icing (4oz)
Salmon pink food colour

25.5 and 35.5cm round cake
 boards (10 and 14in)
Piping tubes No.1 and 2
Cocktail stick
Assorted floral sprays
Board edge ribbon

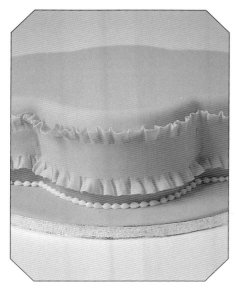

1 Cover the cakes and boards with sugarpaste. Leave until dry. Pipe shells around cake-base (No.2) with royal icing. Cut out, frill and fix sugarpaste strips to cake-side.

2 Frill and fix a narrower sugarpaste band around the cake-side.

3 Pipe floral design as shown, with royal icing (No.1).

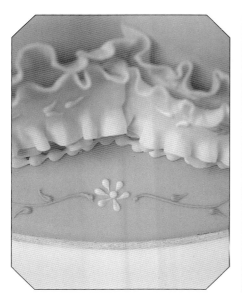

4 Pipe a floral design onto the cake board (No.1).

5 Pipe the curved lines and flowers around the cake-top edge (No.1).

6 Make and fix floral sprays as required. Fix ribbon around the cake board edge.

# BEAUTIFUL PEACH

**1** Cover the cakes and boards with sugarpaste. Cut out a sugarpaste Garret frill. Flute the edge with a cocktail stick. Make the holes shown with piping tube No.3.

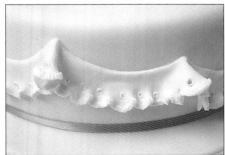

**2** Cut frill and fix, in falling and rising loops around cake-side, making as many frills as required. Pipe lines around holes and then pipe a rope line along edge of each frill (No.1).

**3** Pipe shells along the top edge of each frill (No.1). Pipe decorative floral lines (No.1) then carefully paint over the floral lines with food colour.

25.5, 20.5 and 15cm round
 fruit cakes (10, 8 and 6in)
2.5k almond paste (5lb)
3.5k sugarpaste (7lb)
225g royal icing (8oz)
225g modelling paste (8oz)
Peach food colour

35.5, 25.5 and 20.5cm round
 cake boards (14, 10 and 8in)
Garrett frill cutter
Piping tubes No.1 and 3
Flower cutters
Calyx cutter
Fine paint brush

Floral wire and tape
Stamens
75mm wide decorette ribbon (3in)
8mm wide satin ribbon (⅜in)
Ball shaped modelling tool
Board edge ribbon

**4** To make a flower: Cut out petal shape shown from modelling paste. Curl up tip of each petal working from the point of the petal to the base, with a modelling tool.

**5** Form a Mexican hat shape, place cutter over the point and cut the petals. Curl up the end of each petal.

**6** Tape stamens to wire and thread through the two sets of petals and fix as shown. Make as many as required.

**7** To make an Azalea: Form a Mexican hat shape, place cutter over the point and cut the petals.

**8** Frill the edge of each petal with a cocktail stick. Then indent the centre of the flower.

**9** Tape stamens to wire and thread through flower and fix. Paint faint marks on petals with a fine paint brush. Make as many as required. Fix flowers together with ribbons, then to the cakes.

# HARMONY

INGREDIENTS

15, 20.5 and 25.5cm square
 fruit cakes (6, 8 and 10in)
3.5k almond paste (7lb)
3.5k royal icing (7lb)
Assorted food colours

EQUIPMENT and DECORATIONS

20.5, 25.5 and 35.5cm
 square cake boards
 (8, 10 and 14in)
Piping tubes No.1, 2, 3 and 43
Assorted wedding cake favours
Board edge ribbon

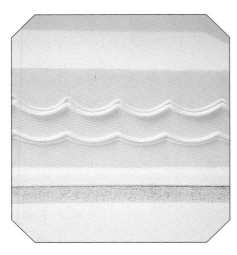

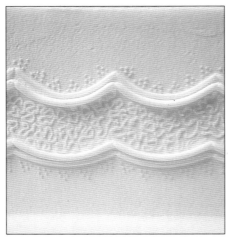

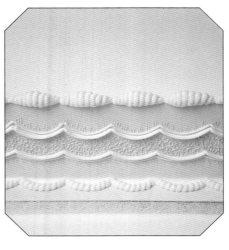

1 Coat cakes and board with royal icing. When dry, pipe two sets of curved lines around cake sides (No.3). Pipe a line above the top line and then below bottom line (No.2).

2 Pipe filigree between the lines (No.1) and dots as shown (No.1).

3 Pipe curved rope lines along the cake-top edge and board (No.43).

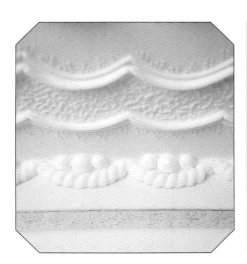

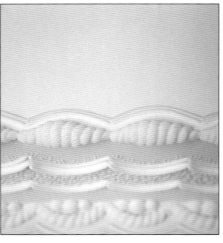

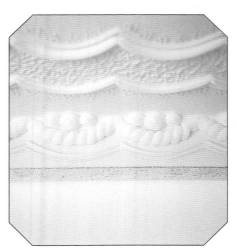

4 Pipe graduated dots around the cake-base (No.2.)

5 Pipe a line beside the cake-top rope line (No.2) then pipe a line beside the No.2 line (No.1).

6 Pipe a line beside the board rope line (No.2) then pipe a line beside the No.2 line (No.1). Fix decorations of choice.

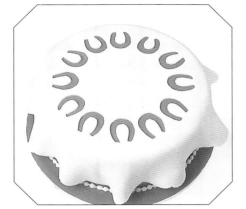

1 Cover cakes and boards with sugarpaste. Pipe shells around cake-base (No.2). Leave to dry for 24 hours. Cover cakes with a second layer of sugarpaste forming a cloth, then cut out horseshoe shapes.

2 When the sugarpaste has dried, pipe dots to form flowers over each cake (No.1).

3 Make and fix floral sprays as required.

INGREDIENTS

15, 20.5 and 25.5cm round
 fruit cakes (6, 8 and 10in)
2.5k almond paste (5lb)
4.5k sugarpaste (9lb)
225g royal icing (8oz)
Blue food colour

EQUIPMENT and DECORATIONS

20.5, 25.5 and 33cm round
 cake boards (8, 10 and 13in)
Piping tubes No.1 and 2
Assorted floral sprays
Board edge ribbon

# CLOUD NINE

## INGREDIENTS

15, 20.5 and 25.5cm
 hexagonal shaped fruit
 cakes (6, 8 and 10in)
3k almond paste (6lb)
3.5k sugarpaste (7lb)
225g modelling paste (8oz)
225g royal icing (8oz)
Assorted food colours

## EQUIPMENT and DECORATIONS

35.5cm hexagonal shaped
 cake board (14in)
15 and 20.5cm hexagonal
 shaped cake cards (6 and 8in)
Blossom cutters
Flower cutters
Leaf cutters
Piping tube No.2
Lace arch
Gold cord
Board edge ribbon

1 Cover each cake with sugarpaste. Stack together, fixing a cake card between each layer. Fix to cake board then cover board edge with sugarpaste. Pipe shells around each base (No.2) with royal icing.

2 Cut out and fix sugarpaste Edelweiss to a number of corners.

3 Cut out and fix sugarpaste King of the Alps to a number of corners.

4 Cut out and fix sugarpaste Alpine Roses to the remaining corners.

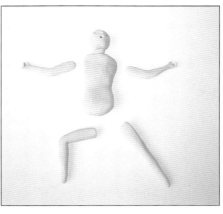

5 Mould the various parts of the bride with sugarpaste.

6 Fix the pieces to the cake-side then cover with sugarpaste dress and climbing boots.

7 Make and fix sugarpaste arms and veil then paint in the hair.

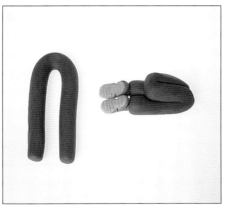

8 Mould a long sugarpaste roll, fold into a kneeling position then make and fix climbing boots.

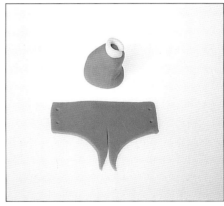

9 Mould the body then cover with sugarpaste wedding jacket.

10 Fix to the legs then make and fix arms and head. Paint in the hair.

11 Fix the groom onto the cake-top, then add gold cord linking to the bride. Make and fix sugarpaste top hat.

12 Fix and decorate the lace arch as shown.

# CHRISTMAS PUDDING

## INGREDIENTS

Chocolate sponge cake baked
 in a 1.2Lt pudding basin (2pt)
1.25k sugarpaste (2½lb)
Brown dusting powder
Assorted food colours

## EQUIPMENT and DECORATIONS

25.5cm round cake board (10in)
Holly leaf cutter
Ball shaped modelling tool

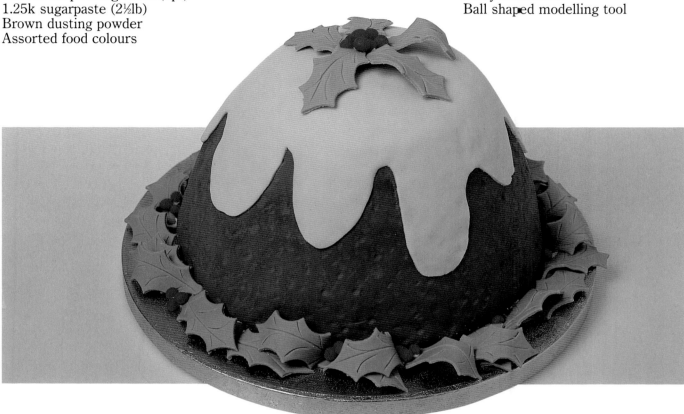

**1** Upturn the sponge cake and cover with sugarpaste. Mark with a ball tool and brush with dusting powder to form texture shown.

**2** Cut and fix sugarpaste custard.

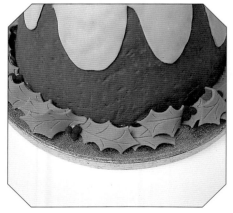

**3** Cut and fix sugarpaste holly leaves and berries around the cake-base and top.

# CHRISTMAS CRACKER

INGREDIENTS

2 swiss rolls
900g sugarpaste (2lb)
115g royal icing (4oz)
Assorted food colours

EQUIPMENT and DECORATIONS

30.5cm round Christmas cake card (12in)
Piping tubes No.1 and 57
Motto and decorations
Cocktail stick

1 Cut one swiss roll in half. Then cover each piece, together with the full swiss roll, with sugarpaste. Make sugarpaste frills and fix together as shown.

2 Decorate the cracker with sugarpaste cut-outs and then pipe the edge with royal icing (No.57).

3 Make and decorate a selection of sugarpaste figures and parcels.

# EVERGREEN

## INGREDIENTS

20.5cm square fruit cake (8in)
900g almond paste (2lb)
900g royal icing (2lb)
Yellow, caramel, green and red
 food colours

## EQUIPMENT and DECORATIONS

25.5cm square cake board (10in)
Holly stencil or plain card
Piping tubes No.1, 2 and 42
Step shaped palette knife
Wide ribbon
Gold bells

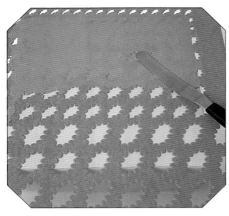

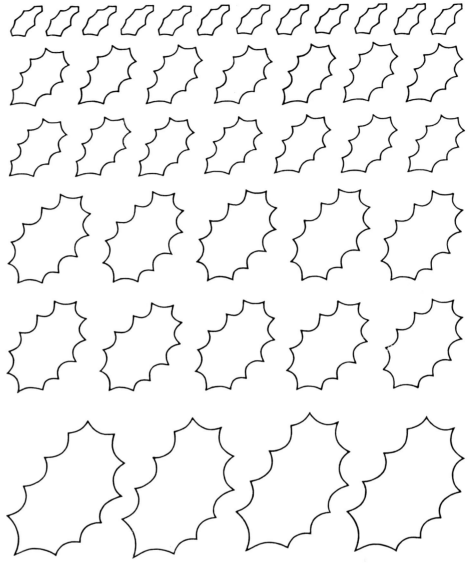

1 Coat cake and board with royal icing. Leave until dry. Using template as a guide, cut out holly leaf shapes from card or use a readymade stencil. Place over cake-top and spread with royal icing.

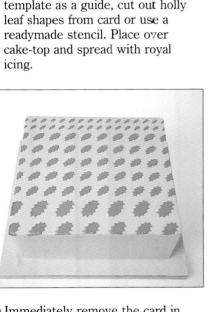

2 Immediately remove the card in one continuous movement.

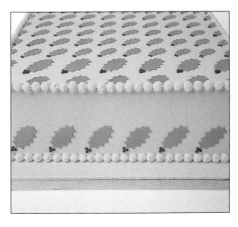

3 Using part of the card repeat process around the cake-base. Pipe berries on each leaf (No.1).

4 Pipe shells along the cake-top edge and base (No.42).

5 Cut and fix ribbon to the cake-top as shown. Pipe message of choice (No.2). Fix the bells to the ribbon.

# SANTA'S SLEIGH

INGREDIENTS

20.5cm square fruit cake (8in)
900g almond paste (2lb)
2k sugarpaste (4lb)
Assorted food colours

EQUIPMENT and DECORATIONS

40.5cm round cake board (16in)
Star shaped cutter
Fancy shaped cutter
Floral wire
Thin card

Christmas glitter
Decorative seasonal spray
Christmas motto
Board edge ribbon

1 Cut the cake in half. Trim to shape shown then cover with sugarpaste.

2 Cover the board with sugarpaste then fix the cakes together to form the sleigh. Cut out and fix sugarpaste stars.

3 Cut out and fix sugarpaste strips to the sleigh as shown.

4 Cut out and fix decorative sugarpaste shapes to the sides of the sleigh. Cut out and fix the runners.

5 Make and fix various sugarpaste toy shapes and Father Christmas.

6 Using the template as a guide, cut out reindeers from card and spray with glitter. Fix to wire then to board as shown in main picture.

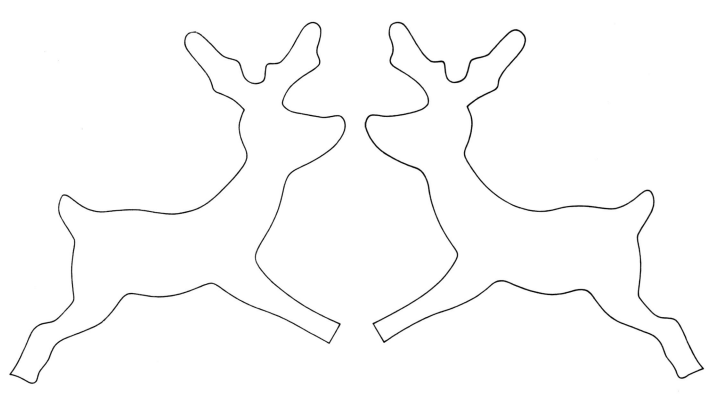

6 miniature sponge cakes or
  2 swiss rolls cut into 6
1.5k sugarpaste (3lb)
225g royal icing (8oz)
Icing sugar for stiffening
Assorted food colours

10cm round cake card (4in)
  6 required
Piping tube No.1
Coarse cloth for marking
Crimper
Ribbon
Doyleys

**1** **To make a sack:** Roll out sugar-paste, mark with a coarse cloth, upturn and place cake on top. Fold the paste up over the cake and seal with a little cooled, boiled water.

**2** Squeeze the neck together then tie with ribbon. Make a small tag and pipe "toys" with royal icing (No.1).

**3** **To make Father Christmas:** cover the cake with sugarpaste then fix a separate piece for the face.

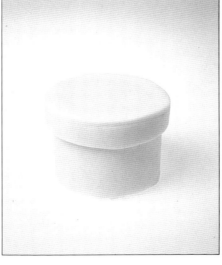

**4** Cut out and fix the hat and bobble, eyes, nose and mouth. Pipe the pupil's with royal icing (No.1).

**5** **To make a gift box:** cover the side of the cake with sugarpaste, make and fix a rim then cover the top.

**6** Cut out and fix sugarpaste strips and bows to the cake-top.

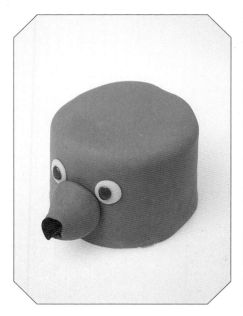

7 **To make a reindeer:** cover a cake with sugarpaste, then make and fix the nose and eyes. Pipe the pupils with royal icing (No.1).

8 Mould the antlers with sugarpaste stiffened with icing sugar and fix to the head together with the ears.

9 **To make a Christmas pudding:** roll out sugarpaste, add small pieces to represent currants and roll in. Then cover a cake. Cut and fix a second layer for sauce effect.

10 Cut out a sugarpaste plate, fix on the cake, then crimp the edge. Make and fix sugarpaste holly and berries.

11 **To make a snowman:** cover a cake with sugarpaste. Make and fix a sugarpaste scarf. Pipe the buttons with royal icing (No.1).

12 Make a head with a small cake covered with sugarpaste. Fix the head, then make and fix the arms. Decorate as shown.

# CHRISTMAS TRADITION

## INGREDIENTS

20.5cm round fruit cake (8in)
680g almond paste (1¼lb)
680g royal icing (1¼lb)
Red and green food colours

## EQUIPMENT and DECORATIONS

28cm petal shaped
  cake board (11in)
Patterned scraper

Piping tubes No.1, 2 and 3
Christmas spray and motto
Board edge ribbon

**1** Coat cake and board with royal icing, using a patterned scraper for cake-side. Pipe bulbs around cake-top edge and base (No.3).

**2** When dry, pipe holly leaves and berries onto each bulb, around the middle of cake-side and onto the board as shown (No.1).

**3** Stipple cake-top with royal icing, leaving a circle in the middle. Pipe pointed bulbs around edge of the circle (No.2). Fix the spray and motto.

# YULETIDE LANTERN

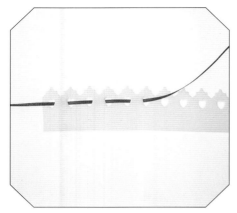

**1** Cut out two colours of sugarpaste, using template as a guide, to form lantern shapes. Leave until dry.

**2** When lanterns are dry, cover cake with sugarpaste, gently push out small size lantern shape, then insert as shown.

**3** Cut out sugarpaste strips, using the continuous cutter, then thread ribbon through the holes as shown.

## INGREDIENTS

20.5cm diamond shaped fruit cake (8in)
900g almond paste (2lb)
1.25k sugarpaste (2½lb)
225g royal icing (8oz)
Coloured granulated sugar
Assorted food colours

## EQUIPMENT and DECORATIONS

30.5cm diamond shaped cake board (12in)
Continuous cutter
Narrow ribbon
Piping tubes No.1 and 2
Non-stick paper
Blossom cutter
Board edge ribbon

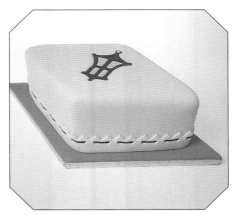

$4$ Fix the strips to the cake-base.

$5$ Pipe paper chain pattern and the glow lines (No.1).

$6$ Pipe bell shapes using royal icing without glycerin, onto non-stick paper (No.2). Sprinkle with coloured granulated sugar, leave until half dry then scoop out centres and fix to cake-top corners.

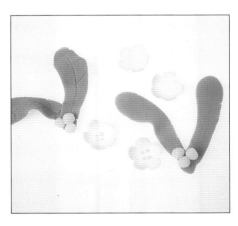

$7$ Make and fix a selection of sugarpaste mistletoe and flowers to the cake board corners.

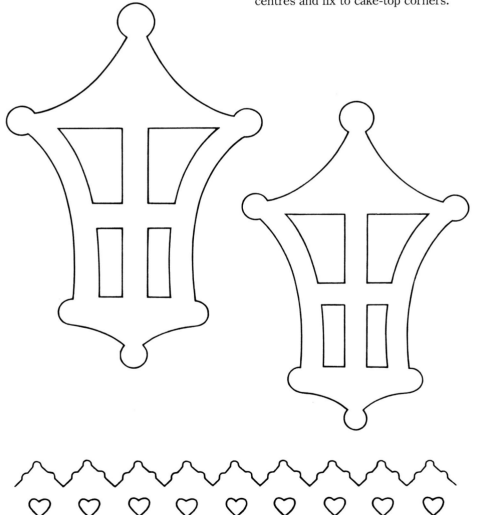

$8$ Pipe yuletide with royal icing (No.1). Fix ribbon around the cake board.

# CHRISTMAS FUN

### INGREDIENTS

20.5cm square sponge cake
 (8in) 2 required
900g sugarpaste (2lb)
450g royal icing (1lb)
225g modelling paste (8oz)
Broken meringue pieces
Assorted food colours

### EQUIPMENT and DECORATIONS

33cm round cake board (13in)
Fine paint brush
Piping tube No.1
Board edge ribbon

1 Cover cake and board with sugarpaste. Using templates as a guide, cut out figure from modelling paste and, when dry, colour as shown. Stipple with royal icing for the snow.

2 Using the template as a guide, cut out figure and, when dry, colour as shown. Stipple with royal icing for the snow.

3 Using the template as a guide, cut out figure and, when dry, colour as shown. Make and colour as many figures as required.

4 Fix broken meringue pieces around the cake-base and cover with royal icing. Then fix in the cut-out figures.

5 Fix cut-outs to the cake-top and then pipe lines shown (No.1).

6 Stipple the cake-top edge with royal icing. Pipe inscription of choice (No.1).

# SNOWFALL

## INGREDIENTS

20.5cm round fruit cake (8in)
680g almond paste (1½lb)
680g royal icing (1½lb)
Assorted food colours

## EQUIPMENT and DECORATIONS

30.5cm round cake board (12in)
Serrated scraper
Fine paint brush

Piping tubes No.1 and 4
Seasonal decorations
Board edge ribbon

 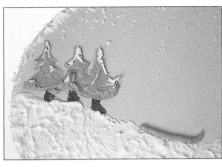 

**1** Place cake onto board into position shown. Coat with royal icing using a serrated scraper. When dry, stipple with royal icing to form snow effect shown.

**2** Roughly brush royal icing to form the trees as shown. Pipe the sleigh (No.4). Stipple snowflakes with a paint brush.

**3** Pipe and decorate the snowmen as shown (No.4 and 1). Then fix seasonal decorations to the board.

# CHRISTMAS TREE ROBINS

INGREDIENTS

20.5cm square sponge cake (8in)
450g buttercream (1lb)
225g sugarpaste (8oz)
Green, brown and red food colours

EQUIPMENT and DECORATIONS

25.5cm round Christmas cake card
Paint brush
Assorted Christmas cake decorations

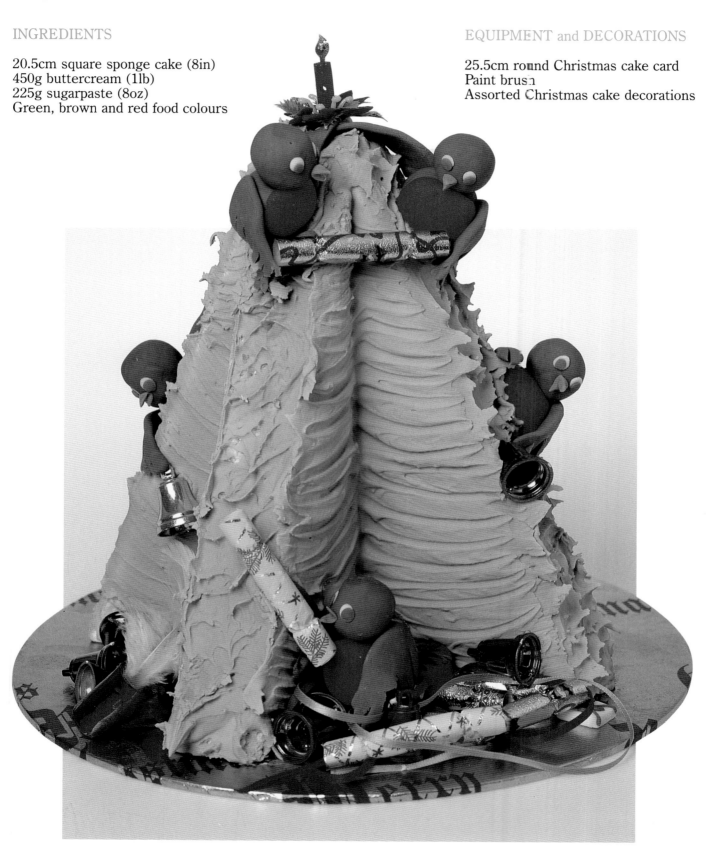

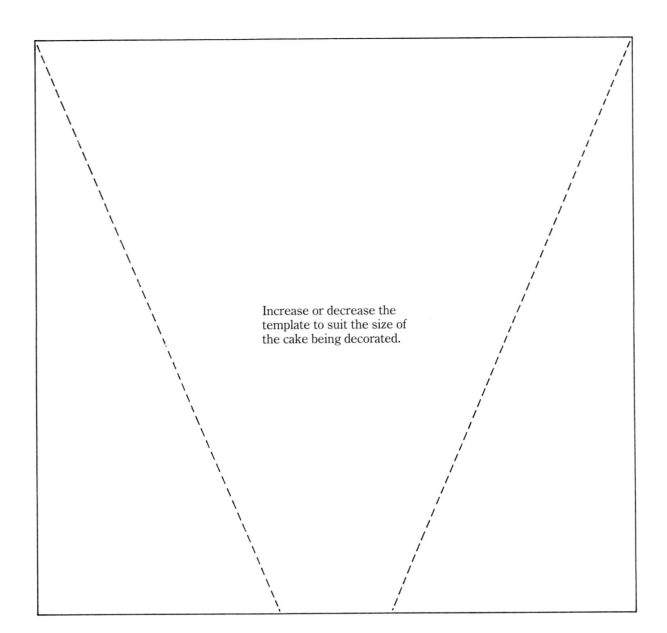

Increase or decrease the
template to suit the size of
the cake being decorated.

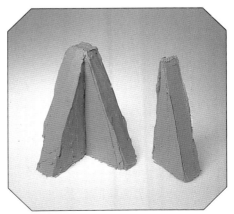

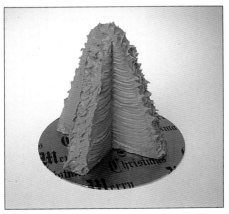

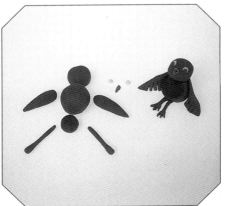

**1** Using the template as a guide, cut the sponge into three pieces. Coat each piece with buttercream and fix together to form a tree.

**2** Fix the tree to the cake card then brush on additional buttercream to form effect shown.

**3** Mould the various parts of a sugarpaste robin and fix together. Make as many robins as required then fix to the tree with the other decorations.

# MERRY CHRISTMAS

1 Cover the cake and board with sugarpaste then crimp the cake-top edge and board. Paint holly leaves and berries around the cake-side.

2 Pipe shells with royal icing around the cake-base (No.43).

3 Cut out and decorate a sugarpaste Father Christmas and tree as shown.

4 Cut out and decorate various sugarpaste parcels.

5 Fix the tree, Father Christmas and parcels as required.

20.5cm round sponge (8in)   30.5cm round cake board (12in)
 2 required         Crimper
1.5k sugarpaste (3lb)     Fine paint brush
115g royal icing (4oz)     Piping tubes No.1 and 43
Assorted food colours     Christmas motto

# INDEX AND GLOSSARY

**Cake-base. Where the bottom edges of the cake meet the cake board.**

**Cake card. A thin cake board**

**Coated cake. A cake coated with buttercream or royal icing.**

**Colouring**
**– Almond paste. Fold and mix colour into the almond paste.**
**– Buttercream. Mix colour into the buttercream after it has been made.**
**– Granulated sugar. Carefully add edible food colour to the sugar, mix thoroughly. Allow to dry for 24 hours.**
**– Modelling paste. Fold and mix the colour into the paste.**
**– Mottled paste. Where colouring is not fully mixed into the medium being used.**
**– Piping gel. Stir the colour into the gel.**
**– Royal icing. Mix colour into the royal icing after it has been made. Do not add blue to whiten the icing if pastel shades are required.**
**– Sugarpaste. Fold and mix the colour into the paste.**

**Covered cake. A cake covered with almond paste or sugarpaste**

**Decorative board covering can be wallpaper samples, or patterned paper, glued to the cake board. Use a cake card between the covering and the cake.**

**Embossing. Press an embossing tool, or button with raised pattern, into sugarpaste before the paste is dry.**

**Favours. Small cake decorations.**

**Filigree. Piping irregular lines whilst keeping the piping tube on the cake surface.**

**Frills. To make frills, place tapered end of a cocktail stick, or paint brush handle, over the edge of thinly rolled sugarpaste or modelling paste, and rock it back and forth a little at a time.**

**Leaf bag. A piping bag with the tip cut to a 'V' shape.**

**Leave to dry. Leave to dry in a temperature of 18°C (65°F).**

**In a high humidity a longer time may be needed than stated.**

**Modelling paste. Used for cut-out figures or items that need to stand alone as it is stronger than sugarpaste. Fix to cake with royal icing.**

**Non-stick paper. Specially prepared paper for figure piping and flood-in work.**

**Overpipe. To repeat the same pattern on existing piping.**

**Pipe-in. To pipe medium in use without a piping tube in the piping bag.**

**Stencils.** These are easily available from many craft shops. To make, trace design onto card. Cut out with scalpel or sharp knife. Place onto cake. Carefully spread softened royal icing over the stencil. Scrape off surplus with palette knife. Peel the stencil off in one continuous movement.

**Stippling.** Royal icing, or buttercream, should be stippled with a dry sponge or palette knife.

**Templates.** An aid for designs. To transfer templates:
1. Cut out card templates in sections. Place on cake-top and pipe around sections with royal icing. When dry, carefully remove the pieces. OR
2. Trace template onto greaseproof paper with a food-approved pen. Place design onto the cake-top. With a sharp pointed tool, press along the lines to leave an impression. OR
3. Retrace lines on back of design. Turn paper over and place on cake-top. Trace over with food-approved pen.

# PIPING TUBES and SHAPES

The diagram shows the icing tube shapes used in this book. Please note that these are Mary Ford tubes, but comparable tubes may be used.

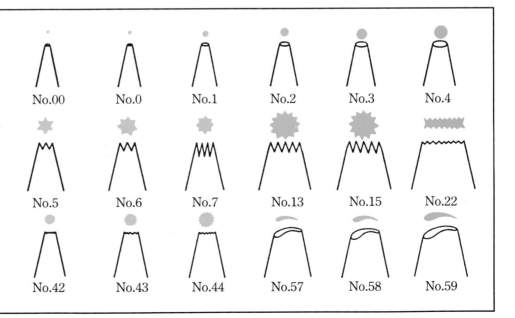

No.00 No.0 No.1 No.2 No.3 No.4
No.5 No.6 No.7 No.13 No.15 No.22
No.42 No.43 No.44 No.57 No.58 No.59

## 101 Cake Designs
ISBN: 0 946429 00 6                                      320 pages
The original Mary Ford cake artistry text book. A classic in its field, over 200,000 copies sold.

## Cake Making and Decorating
ISBN: 0 946429 41 3                                       96 pages
Mary Ford divulges all the skills and techniques cake decorators need to make and decorate a variety of cakes in every medium.

## Jams, Chutneys and Pickles
ISBN: 0 946429 48 0                                       96 pages
Over 70 of Mary Ford's favourite recipes for delicious jams, jellies, pickles and chutneys with hints and tips for perfect results.

## Children's Cakes
ISBN: 0 946429 35 9                                       96 pages
33 exciting new Mary Ford designs and templates for children's cakes in a wide range of mediums.

## Children's Birthday Cakes
ISBN: 0 946429 46 4                                      112 pages
The book to have next to you in the kitchen! Over forty new cake ideas for children's cakes with an introduction on cake making and baking to ensure the cake is both delicious as well as admired.

## Party Cakes
ISBN: 0 946429 13 8                                      120 pages
36 superb party time sponge cake designs and templates for tots to teenagers. An invaluable prop for the party cake decorator.

## Quick and Easy Cakes
ISBN: 0 946429 42 1                                      208 pages
The book for the busy mum. 99 new ideas for party and special occasion cakes.

## Decorative Sugar Flowers for Cakes
ISBN: 0 946429 51 0                                      120 pages
33 of the highest quality handcrafted sugar flowers with cutter shapes, background information and appropriate uses.

## Wedding Cakes
ISBN: 0 946429 39 1                                       96 pages
For most cake decorators, the wedding cake is the most complicated item they will produce. This book gives a full step-by-step description of the techniques required and includes over 20 new cake designs.

## Sugarcraft Cake Decorating
ISBN: 0 946429 30 8                                       96 pages
A definitive sugarcraft book featuring an extensive selection of exquisite sugarcraft items designed and made by Pat Ashby.

## Cake Recipes
ISBN: 0 946429 43 X                                       96 pages
Contains 60 of Mary's favourite cake recipes ranging from fruit cake to cinnamon crumble cake.

## Home Baking with Chocolate
ISBN: 0 946429 37 5                                       96 pages
Over 60 tried and tested recipes for cakes, gateaux, biscuits, confectionery and desserts. The ideal book for busy mothers.

## Making Cakes for Money
ISBN: 0 946429 44 8                                      120 pages
The complete guide to making and costing cakes for sale at stalls or to friends. Invaluable advice on costing ingredients and time accurately.

## The Complete Book of Cake Decorating
ISBN: 0 946429 36 7                                      256 pages
An indispensable reference book for cake decorators, containing totally new material covering every aspect of cake design and artistry.

## The Beginners Guide to Cake Decorating
ISBN: 0 946429 38 3                                      256 pages
A comprehensive guide for the complete beginner to every stage of the cake decorating process, including over 150 cake designs for different occasions.

## Desserts
ISBN: 0 946429 40 5                                       96 pages
Hot and cold desserts suitable for every occasion, using fresh, natural ingredients. An invaluable reference book for the home cook, chef or student.

## The New Book of Cake Decorating
ISBN: 0 9462429 45 6                                      224 pages
The most comprehensive title in the Mary Ford list. It includes over 100 new cake designs and full descriptions of all the latest techniques.

## BOOKS BY MAIL ORDER

Mary Ford operates a mail order service for all her step-by-step titles. If you write to Mary at the address below she will provide you with a price list and details. In addition, all names on the list receive information on new books and special offers. Mary is delighted, if required, to write a personal message in any book purchased by mail order.

Write to:   Mary Ford,
            30 Duncliff Road,
            Southbourne, Bournemouth,
            Dorset. BH6 4LJ. U.K.